STANDARDS FOR
Reading Professionals

REVISED 2010

INTERNATIONAL
READING
ASSOCIATION

A Reference FOR THE Preparation OF Educators IN THE United States

INTERNATIONAL
READING ASSOCIATION
800 BARKSDALE ROAD, PO BOX 8139
NEWARK, DE 19714-8139, USA
www.reading.org

The International Reading Association attempts, through its publications, to provide a forum for a wide spectrum of opinions on reading. This policy permits divergent viewpoints without implying the endorsement of the Association.

Executive Editor, Books   Corinne M. Mooney
Developmental Editor   Charlene M. Nichols
Developmental Editor   Tori Mello Bachman
Developmental Editor   Stacey L. Reid
Editorial Production Manager   Shannon T. Fortner
Design and Composition Manager   Anette Schuetz

Project Editors   Stacey L. Reid and Susanne Viscarra

Cover Design   Adam Bohannon

Library of Congress Cataloging-in-Publication Data

Standards for reading professionals—revised 2010.

   p. cm.

   Developed by the Professional Standards and Ethics Committee of the International Reading Association.
   Includes bibliographical references.
   ISBN 978-0-87207-713-3 (alk. paper)
   1. Reading teachers—Training of—Standards—United States. I. International Reading Association. Professional Standards and Ethics Committee.
   LB2844.1.R4S8313 2010   428.4071—dc22

                                                                                                   2010021439

Suggested APA Reference

International Reading Association. (2010). *Standards for reading professionals—revised 2010*. Newark, DE: Author.

Contact Information

International Reading Association
Research and Professional Development
800 Barksdale Road, PO Box 8139
Newark, DE 19714-8139
302-731-1600, ext. 226 • 302-731-1057 (fax)
gkeating@reading.org • www.reading.org

Contents

The International Reading Association Standards 2010 Committee

IRA would like to thank the following members of the Standards 2010 Committee for their work on this document.

Rita M. Bean (chair)
University of Pittsburgh, Pennsylvania

Maryann M. Manning (Board liaison)
University of Alabama, Tuscaloosa

Cathy Roller
International Reading Association,
Newark, Delaware

Jennifer L. Altieri
The Citadel,
Charleston, South Carolina

Marino C. Alvarez
Tennessee State University, Nashville

Betsy Baker-Rall
Parkade Elementary School,
Columbia, Missouri

Camille L. Blachowicz
National-Louis University,
Chicago, Illinois

Deborah E. Bordelon
Governors State University,
University Park, Illinois

Jack Cassidy
Texas A&M University, Corpus Christi

Darion M. Griffin
American Federation of Teachers,
Washington, DC

James V. Hoffman
University of Texas, Austin

Laveria F. Hutchison
University of Houston, Texas

Barbara A. Kapinus
National Education Association,
Washington, DC

Jacqueline C. Karbon
Wisconsin Department of Public
Instruction, Milwaukee

Diane Kern
University of Rhode Island, Kingston

Barbara Laster
Towson University, Maryland

Evan B. Lefsky
Lake County Schools, Tavares, Florida

Debra A. Miller
McDaniel College,
Westminster, Maryland

Lesley Mandel Morrow
Rutgers, The State University
of New Jersey, New Brunswick

Victoria J. Risko
Vanderbilt University,
Nashville, Tennessee

Kathleen Roskos
John Carroll University,
University Heights, Ohio

Michael L. Shaw
St. Thomas Aquinas College,
Sparkill, New York

Allison Skerrett
University of Texas, Austin

William Earl Smith
Ohio University, Athens

Dorothy S. Strickland
Rutgers, The State University
of New Jersey, New Brunswick

Alfred W. Tatum
University of Illinois at Chicago

Corinne C. Valadez
Texas A&M University, Corpus Christi

Acknowledgments

*S*tandards for Reading Professionals—Revised 2010 was developed by the representative Standards 2010 Committee, appointed by the International Reading Association (IRA) to revise the 2003 document. Committee members represented many different institutions, regions of the country, and views about the roles and responsibilities of literacy professionals.

The Committee worked tirelessly for three years, debating various issues about the roles of literacy professions. They agreed—and disagreed—but as reflected in a variation of a Japanese proverb, "None of us is as strong as all of us," they were able to come to a consensus that resulted in this document. We acknowledge and thank the Committee members for their contributions to this 2010 revision. We also want to recognize the special efforts of those who served as chairs of the subcommittees: Kathy Roskos (John Carroll University, Ohio), Diane Kern (University of Rhode Island), Debra Miller (McDaniel College, Maryland), James Hoffman (University of Texas), Betsy Baker-Rall from Missouri, and Evan Lefsky (Lake County Schools, Florida).

Special appreciation is extended also to the following individuals:

- Cathy Roller, former Director of Research, IRA, for her leadership during this process

- Gail Keating, Projects Manager, Research and Professional Development, IRA, for facilitating the work of the committee, her attention to detail, asking the important questions, and her diligence in making certain that the document reflected the decisions made by the Committee

- Rita Bean, University of Pittsburgh, for chairing the Committee and facilitating meetings that provided opportunities for all voices to be heard

Finally, we express our gratitude to the many literacy professionals and groups who provided important feedback to the Committee by attending sessions at the IRA conferences, responding to the drafts of the Standards on the IRA website, and talking with Committee members informally. The Committee sought to reflect the many voices, interests, and concerns of our constituents and produce a document that will assist in preparing reading professionals for the schools of today and tomorrow.

Introduction

About *Standards 2010*

Standards for Reading Professionals—Revised 2010 (*Standards 2010*) sets forth the criteria for developing and evaluating preparation programs for reading professionals. The Standards describe what candidates for the reading profession should know and be able to do in professional settings. The Standards are performance based, focusing on the knowledge, skills, and dispositions necessary for effective educational practice in a specific role. Also, the Standards are the result of a deliberative process that drew from professional expertise and research in the reading field.

In this Introduction, a description of the major changes between these Standards and those in *Standards 2003* is provided, followed by an overview of *Standards 2010*.

Issues in Reading Education

Part 4 provides detailed information about the issues and topics addressed by the Standards 2010 Committee in preparing this document. We suggest that users of this document read this section before they begin to work with the Standards and elements. The information in this section can help readers gain a better understanding of the issues faced by the Committee and the rationale underlying their decisions.

Major Changes in *Standards 2010*

While *Standards 2010* maintains the performance-based emphasis of *Standards 2003*, four significant changes are described as follows.

Professional Role Categories

The number of professional role categories was increased from five in *Standards 2003* to seven in *Standards 2010*. The two additional roles are (1) the Middle and High School Classroom Teacher (academic content teacher) and (2) the Middle and High School Reading Classroom Teacher. Thus, there are three categories of classroom teacher: pre-K and elementary, middle and high school content, and middle and high school reading. These three categories allow for specificity that captures the differences in the various classroom teacher roles.

In addition, *Paraprofessional* was changed to *Education Support Personnel* in *Standards 2010* to reflect the title currently being used in the field.

Organization by Standard and Then by Role

Standards are first presented as in the *Standards 2003* document; that is, a standard is presented across all roles (see pages 18–33) in a matrix that has the roles listed as column heads and the particular standard's elements listed in the left column as one element per row. This matrix design enables readers to recognize the differences in expectations among the professional roles.

However, *Standards 2010* also provides matrixes that list each role individually with the accompanying elements of each of the standards (see pages 35–60), which allows readers to look either at a specific standard's element and its description across all roles, or at a role, such as Reading Specialist/Literacy Coach, to see what the Standards require for that specific role. Programs submitting reports to IRA must focus on meeting Standards at the Reading Specialist/Literacy Coach role (see pages 49–54).

Change From Performance Indicators to List of "Possible Evidence"

In *Standards 2003*, the Standards' elements were accompanied by lists of performance indicators per role, which were used to build and evaluate programs. Program committees often felt it necessary to require assignments or demonstrate accomplishment of each of the performance indicators when submitting a program for review. In *Standards 2010*, we provide lists of indicators that reflect the intent of an element, but we emphasize that the lists provide possible sources of evidence and that there may be other means of demonstrating competency; more important, it is unnecessary for a program to demonstrate accomplishment of each of the indicators in the lists. However, it is essential that programs include evidence of coaching competence for the Reading Specialist/Literacy Coach role.

Diversity Standard Added

Standards 2010 addresses diversity in a separate standard, Standard 4, given the critical need for preparing reading professionals to teach effectively the diverse student population in schools today. The achievement gaps between white and other minority groups, between those whose primary language is English and English learners, or between students who come from low or high socioeconomic groups, for example, speak to the need to prepare professionals to be effective in working with all students.

Description of *Standards 2010*

The six standards in this document are:

- Standard 1: Foundational Knowledge
- Standard 2: Curriculum and Instruction
- Standard 3: Assessment and Evaluation
- Standard 4: Diversity
- Standard 5: Literate Environment
- Standard 6: Professional Learning and Leadership

Standards Matrix

Each standard is defined by elements that provide more specificity as to the content of that standard. As mentioned previously, the document includes possible sources of evidence for each element that may be used to develop activities or assignments or evaluate specific preparation programs. The elements and indicators in the Evidence (roles) columns have been revised to reflect advances in the reading field. For example, given the importance of technology in reading and writing instruction, we highlight ways in which reading professionals can demonstrate their competence with these new literacies.

The Standards also reflect increased attention to English learners, given the increase in numbers of such students in schools and advances in knowledge about how to successfully provide literacy instruction for them. *Standards 2010* also highlights elements and indicators that describe more specifically the various roles of the Reading Specialist/Literacy Coach.

Assumptions

In the text preceding the Standards matrixes in Part 1, we also include a list of assumptions for each standard as well as a list of references that may be useful to users of this document. The assumptions were developed by Standards 2010 Committee members based on review of the research to serve as a foundation and rationale for each of the Standards and were used by the Committee in developing the Standards and their elements.

Research Base and References

The research base for *Standards 2010*, which provides the foundation for the work in this document, is explicated in Part 3. Also, following each standard's discussion in Part 1, there are citations of both empirical research and theoretical and practical pieces that provide more depth and information about the standard. The references help users of this document develop a more accurate and stronger understanding of the Standards and how they are to be applied when planning for and evaluating preparation programs.

A list of IRA publications useful to those working with the Standards is also provided in Appendix C. Some of the publications describe specific research studies related to preparing reading professionals (e.g., Status of Reading Instruction Institute & IRA, 2007).

Role-Based Organization

As noted above, *Standards 2010* adds the role-based organization to make it easier for those who use the Standards to better understand the competencies for each of the seven professional role categories. Personnel responsible for developing or evaluating programs for the Reading Specialist/Literacy Coach role, therefore, may focus on the Standards matrix for that particular role (see pages 49–54). The roles in each section begin with a brief description of the role and the specific experience or programmatic requirements. Then, each standard's elements are presented for a specific role with "possible evidence" about knowledge, skills, and dispositions for that role, along with some explanatory notes.

The seven professional role categories are:

1. Education Support Personnel Candidate
2. Pre-K and Elementary Classroom Teacher Candidate
3. Middle and High School Content Classroom Teacher Candidate

4. Middle and High School Reading Classroom Teacher Candidate
5. Reading Specialist/Literacy Coach Candidate
6. Teacher Educator Candidate
7. Administrator Candidate

Vignettes

In Appendix A are vignettes of two roles that often require candidates to serve multiple functions or for which there is some ambiguity in terms of the perceptions of these roles. Specifically, vignettes for several aspects of the Reading Specialist/Literacy Coach role and the Middle and High School Reading Classroom Teacher role are provided.

Users of *Standards 2010*

Community college, college, and university faculties as well as state department staff use the Standards in planning preparation programs for education support personnel, classroom reading teachers, reading specialists/ literacy coaches, reading teacher educators, and administrators. The Standards are also used as the basis for evaluating both candidates and programs. In addition, the National Council for Accreditation of Teacher Education (NCATE) uses the Standards for the Reading Specialist/Literacy Coach categories in accreditation decisions.

IRA is the specialty professional association (SPA) that conducts reviews of the Reading Specialist/Literacy Coach category for NCATE accreditation (see the NCATE Accreditation section in this Introduction for further information). NCATE also uses the Standards to inform their Reading and Language Arts Elementary Teacher standards. The Standards have similarly influenced and been influenced by the standards related to reading of the Interstate New Teacher Assessment and Support Consortium and the National Board for Professional Teaching Standards (NBPTS).

IRA Standards and Review of Programs

A standards-based approach to professional education depends on two complementary parts: strong standards plus assessments that measure what the standards expect. *Standards 2010* can be used by institutions of higher education, state departments, or other entities to guide the assessment of candidate preparation in reading as well as professional program effectiveness. In this section, we provide basic information about standards–assessment alignment, followed by specific information pertaining to the use of the 2010 Standards in the NCATE accreditation process.

Standards 2010 is grounded in professional expertise and reading research that has identified the performance criteria demonstrated by competent reading professionals. In planning preparation programs, the Standards guide the selection of program content and learning activities that prepare candidates for their respective roles as reading professionals. The Standards are performance based, not course based; thus, they allow flexibility of program design by state licensing boards and higher education institutions. Yet, where appropriate, *Standards 2010* provides guidance as to the number of courses and semester hours that might be included in programs to ensure high-quality performance in each professional role.

To be effective, assessment of candidate performance should be aligned to reading standards. Several important points follow that help to clarify this process when measuring candidate outcomes and program quality by using *Standards 2010*. First, the Standards and their accompanying elements should be the focus of the assessment. *Standards 2010* has no more than four elements per standard. Assessments should attempt to measure content, skills, and dispositions represented in the elements; possible evidence that can be used to assess specific elements is also provided.

A few principles apply. Assessment should (a) measure only content, skills, and disposition reflected in the elements, (b) effectively *sample* the important knowledge and skills of the standard, and (c) measure complex concepts, critical reasoning, and higher level cognitive demands (Rothman, Slattery, Vranek, & Resnick, 2002). Assessment tasks should be well aligned to the elements for each standard in terms of content, performance (cognitive demand), and challenge. The assessment tasks should also reflect balance across the elements and range, such that the elements are adequately covered (Wiggins & McTighe, 2007).

Assessment may take different approaches suited to local program preferences, such as performance based, projects, and portfolios. Tools and activities may be holistic in nature, addressing each element of a standard in creative and integrative ways. One or multiple assessments may be used across standards to collect evidence of performance that meets criteria.

NCATE Accreditation

The Standards for the Reading Specialist/Literacy Coach role are used in decisions regarding accreditation of master's degree programs for Reading Specialists. IRA has been a constituent member of NCATE since 1980. As 1 of 33 SPAs, IRA has developed a strong and positive role within the NCATE coalition. Members of IRA's Professional Standards and Ethics Committee serve as advisors on the IRA–NCATE partnership and, with others, act as program reviewers and auditors. NCATE, in partnership with IRA, awards national recognition to Reading Specialist/Literacy Coach programs that substantially meet professional standards as documented through a performance-based assessment system.

Reading Specialist/Literacy Coach programs that seek national recognition from NCATE and IRA must carefully align program tasks and assessments to IRA's *Standards 2010* at the Reading Specialist/Literacy Coach level. The role of the Reading Specialist/Literacy Coach remains in one column of the Standards matrix, because the Standards expect evidence of both roles— Reading Specialist and Literacy Coach. Programs must also adhere to NCATE requirements and incorporate evidence that meets four principles of the NCATE SPA Standards; these principles are subsumed in *Standards 2010* as follows:

- Principle 1: Content Knowledge (Standard 1)
- Principle 2: Content Pedagogy (Standards 2 and 3)
- Principle 3: Learning Environments (Standards 4 and 5)
- Principle 4: Professional Knowledge and Skills (Standard 6)

NCATE (2010), with its new criteria, indicates that there should be no subdivisions of standards beyond the element level. Thus, for each of these Standards, elements are provided, and then we include a column with possible evidence that may be used for assessment purposes. NCATE will be evaluating programs, therefore, based on the "preponderance of evidence" presented to demonstrate competency. For those institutions participating in an NCATE review, IRA will provide accompanying material, including a rubric that will assist those institutions in preparing their program review materials. (See the IRA website [www.reading.org/Resources/ProfessionalDevelopment/Accreditation/Support.aspx] for model assessments.)

Many supports to institutions preparing for NCATE/IRA reports and site visits are available from NCATE and IRA staff. In addition to sessions at the annual meetings of IRA and the Association of Literacy Educators and Researchers (ALER), current specifications, additional resources, and model program reports are available at www.reading.org/Resources/ProfessionalDevelopment/Accreditation/Support.aspx. Readers can also find examples of assessment tools at this link.

Summary

In conclusion, the document *Standards 2010* is intended to strengthen the field by providing a well organized and specific set of performance criteria to shape preparation programs. The Standards are the result of a deliberative process that involved constant intertwining of research evidence and professional judgment. We expect this document to contribute to an evidence-based practice that ultimately improves student reading achievement.

PART 1

Progression of Standards Across the Roles, Including Assumptions and References

Standard 1: Foundational Knowledge

Candidates understand the theoretical and evidence-based foundations of reading and writing processes and instruction.

Foundational knowledge is at the core of preparing individuals for roles in the reading profession and encompasses the major theories, research, and best practices that share a consensus of acceptance in the reading field. Individuals who enter the reading profession should understand the historically shared knowledge of the profession and develop the capacity to act on that knowledge responsibly. Elements of the Foundational Knowledge Standard set expectations in the domains of theoretical and practical knowledge, and in developing dispositions for the active, ethical use of professional knowledge. Expectations are founded on the concept of a profession as both a technical and moral enterprise, that is, competent performance for the betterment of society.

The following are the major assumptions of the Standards 2010 Committee for developing this standard and its elements:

• Based on several decades of cognitive science research on human learning, knowledge is domain specific and contextualized. Social experience and context play a role in the construction and development of knowledge.

• Knowledge in the reading field includes archival research-based knowledge and practical knowledge that reflects the wisdom of practice.

• Members of a professional community develop the capacity to learn from experience and contemplate their own practices in systematic ways.

• Knowledge represents the currently shared content of the reading field, subject to change over time as new knowledge and understandings are acquired.

Research and Supporting Literature

The content of Standard 1 reflects our understanding of the professional literature in the preparation of individuals for roles in the reading field, and describes the foundational body of knowledge that individuals need to be active participants and contributors in the reading professional community.

The following are representative research and literature consulted by the Standards 2010 Committee in developing this standard:

Anderson, L.W., & Krathwohl, D.R. (Eds.) (2001). *A taxonomy for learning, teaching, and assessing: A revision of Bloom's taxonomy of educational objectives.* New York: Longman.

August, D., & Shanahan, T. (Eds.). (2008). *Developing reading and writing in second-language learners: Lessons from the report of the National Literacy Panel on Language-Minority Children and Youth.* New York: Routledge; Washington, DC: Center for Applied Linguistics; Newark, DE: International Reading Association.

Clay, M.M. (1985). *The early detection of reading difficulties* (3rd ed.). Portsmouth, NH: Heinemann.

Hammerness, K., & Darling-Hammond, L. (with Grossman, P., Rust, F., & Shulman, L.). (2005). The design of teacher education programs. In L. Darling-Hammond & J. Bransford (Eds.), *Preparing teachers for a changing world: What teachers should learn and be able to do* (pp. 390–441). San Francisco: Jossey-Bass.

McKenna, M.C., & Stahl, K.A.D. (2009). *Assessment for reading instruction* (2nd ed.). New York: Guilford.

Pearson, P.D. (2004). American reading education since 1967. In *Preparing reading professionals: A collection from the International Reading Association* (pp. 6–40). Newark, DE: International Reading Association. (Reprinted from *American reading instruction*, pp. 419–486, by N.B. Smith, Ed., 2002, Newark, DE: International Reading Association)

Rosenblatt, L.M. (1994). The transactional theory of reading and writing. In R.B. Ruddell, M.R. Ruddell, & H. Singer (Eds.), *Theoretical models and processes of reading* (4th ed., pp. 1057–1092). Newark, DE: International Reading Association.

Shulman, L.S. (1998). Theory, practice, and the education of professionals. *The Elementary School Journal, 98*(5), 511–526. doi:10.1086/461912

Snow, C.E., Griffin, P., & Burns, M.S. (Eds.). (2005). *Knowledge to support the teaching of reading: Preparing teachers for a changing world.* San Francisco: Jossey-Bass.

Stanovich, P.J., & Stanovich, K.E. (2003). *Using research and reason in education: How teachers can use scientifically based research to make curricular and instructional decisions.* Washington, DC: National Institute for Literacy, U.S. Department of Education.

Status of Reading Instruction Institute & International Reading Association. (2007). *Teaching reading well: A synthesis of the International Reading Association's research on teacher preparation for reading instruction.* Newark, DE: International Reading Association.

Thornton, H. (2006). Dispositions in action: Do dispositions make a difference in practice? *Teacher Education Quarterly, 33*(2), 53–68.

Tracey, D.H., & Morrow, L.M. (2006). *Lenses on reading: An introduction to theories and models.* New York: Guilford.

Vygotsky, L. (1986). *Thought and language* (A. Kozulin, Ed. & Trans., Rev. ed.). Cambridge, MA: MIT Press.

Wiggins, G., & McTighe, J. (2007). *Schooling by design: Mission, action, and achievement.* Alexandria, VA: Association for Supervision and Curriculum Development.

Standard 2: Curriculum and Instruction

Candidates use instructional approaches, materials, and an integrated, comprehensive, balanced curriculum to support student learning in reading and writing.

The Curriculum and Instruction Standard recognizes the need to prepare educators who have a deep understanding and knowledge of the elements of a balanced, integrated, and comprehensive literacy curriculum and have developed expertise in enacting that curriculum. The elements focus on the use of effective practices in a well-articulated curriculum, using traditional print, digital, and online resources.

The following are the major assumptions of the Standards 2010 Committee for developing this standard and its elements:

- Foundational knowledge about literacy is essential in establishing a vision, and developing and enacting an integrated, comprehensive, and balanced curriculum that is responsive to the needs of diverse learners.

- A conceptual framework for literacy development should inform teaching practices and selection of materials.

- Evidence-based instructional strategies and practices should be used in developing and implementing instruction and a balanced and motivating reading and writing program.

- Comprehensive reading programs provide a wide variety of traditional print, digital, and online resources to meet the needs of diverse students.

- Traditional print, digital, and online reading and writing experiences that incorporate multiple genres, multiple perspectives, and media and communication technologies are necessary to prepare learners for literacy tasks of the 21st century.

Research and Supporting Literature

The following are representative research and literature consulted by the Standards 2010 Committee in developing this standard:

Anstey, M., & Bull, G. (2006). *Teaching and learning multiliteracies: Changing times, changing literacies.* Newark, DE: International Reading Association.

Au, K.H. (2002). Balanced literacy instruction: Addressing issues of equity. In C.M. Roller (Ed.), *Comprehensive reading instruction across the grade levels: A collection of papers from the Reading Research 2001 Conference* (pp. 70–87). Newark, DE: International Reading Association.

Bear, D.R., Invernizzi, M., Templeton, S., & Johnston, F. (2007). *Words their way: Word study for phonics, vocabulary, and spelling instruction* (4th ed.). Upper Saddle River, NJ: Prentice Hall.

Beck, I.L., Perfetti, C.A., & McKeown, M.G. (1982). Effects of long-term vocabulary instruction on lexical access and reading comprehension. *Journal of Educational Psychology, 74*(4), 506–521. doi:10.1037/0022-0663.74.4.506

Blachowicz, C., & Fisher, P.J. (2009). *Teaching vocabulary in all classrooms* (4th ed.). Boston: Allyn & Bacon.

Blachowicz, C., & Ogle, D. (2001). *Reading comprehension: Strategies for independent learners.* New York: Guilford.

Coiro, J., & Dobler, E. (2007). Exploring the online reading comprehension strategies used by sixth-grade skilled readers to search for and locate information on the Internet. *Reading Research Quarterly, 42*(2), 214–257. doi:10.1598/RRQ.42.2.2

Coiro, J., Knobel, M., Lankshear, C., & Leu, D.J. (2008). *Handbook of research on new literacies.* Mahwah, NJ: Erlbaum.

Cowen, J.E. (2003). *A balanced approach to beginning reading instruction: A synthesis of six major U.S. research studies*. Newark, DE: International Reading Association.

Dorn, L.J., & Soffos, C. (2005). *Teaching for deep comprehension: A reading workshop approach*. Portland, ME: Stenhouse.

Echevarria, J., Short, D., & Powers, K. (2006). School reform and standards-based education: A model for English-language learners. *The Journal of Educational Research, 99*(4), 195–211. doi:10.3200/JOER.99.4.195-211

Echevarria, J., Vogt, M., & Short, D.J. (2007). *Making content comprehensible for English learners: The SIOP model* (3rd ed.). Boston: Allyn & Bacon.

Farstrup, A.E., & Samuels, S.J. (Eds.). (2002). *What research has to say about reading instruction* (3rd ed.). Newark, DE: International Reading Association.

Farstrup, A.E., & Samuels, S.J. (Eds.). (2008). *What research has to say about vocabulary instruction*. Newark, DE: International Reading Association.

Flood, J., & Anders, P.L. (2005). *Literacy development of students in urban schools: Research and policy*. Newark, DE: International Reading Association.

Flood, J., Lapp, D., Squire, J.R., & Jensen, J.M. (Eds.). (2003). *Handbook of research on teaching the English language arts* (2nd ed.). Mahwah, NJ: Erlbaum.

Fuchs, D., Fuchs, L.S., & Vaughn, S. (2008). *Response to Intervention: A framework for reading educators*. Newark, DE: International Reading Association.

George, P.S. (2005). A rationale for differentiating instruction in the regular classroom. *Theory Into Practice, 44*(3), 185–193. doi:10.1207/s15430421tip4403_2

Hobbs, R. (2007). *Reading the media: Media literacy in high school English*. New York: Teachers College Press.

International Reading Association. (2009). *Response to Intervention: Guiding principles for educators from the International Reading Association* [Brochure]. Newark, DE: Author.

Jetton, T.L., & Dole, J.A. (Eds.). (2004). *Adolescent literacy research and practice*. New York: Guilford.

National Institute of Child Health and Human Development. (2000). *Report of the National Reading Panel. Teaching children to read: An evidence-based assessment of the scientific research literature on reading and its implications for reading instruction* (NIH Publication No. 00-4769). Washington, DC: U.S. Government Printing Office.

Paris, S.G., & Myers, M., II. (1981). Comprehension monitoring, memory, and study strategies of good and poor readers. *Journal of Reading Behavior, 13*(1), 5–22.

Strickland, D.S., & Morrow, L.M. (Eds.). (2000). *Beginning reading and writing*. Newark, DE: International Reading Association; New York: Teachers College Press.

Tomlinson, C.A., & Strickland, C.A. (2005). *Differentiation in practice: A resource guide for differentiating curriculum, grades 9–12*. Alexandria, VA: Association for Supervision and Curriculum Development.

Tyner, B., & Green, S.E. (2005). *Small-group reading instruction: A differentiated teaching model for intermediate readers, grades 3–8*. Newark, DE: International Reading Association.

Standard 3: Assessment and Evaluation

Candidates use a variety of assessment tools and practices to plan and evaluate effective reading and writing instruction.

The Assessment and Evaluation Standard recognizes the need to prepare teachers for using a variety of assessment tools and practices to plan and evaluate effective reading and writing instruction. The elements featured in this standard relate to the systematic monitoring of student performance at individual, classroom, school, and systemwide levels. Teacher educators who specialize in literacy play a critical role in preparing teachers for multifaceted assessment responsibilities.

The following are the major assumptions of the Standards 2010 Committee for developing this standard and its elements:

- The most fundamental goal of assessment and evaluation is to optimize student learning.

- Effective assessment practices inform instruction.

- Competent reading professionals appreciate the importance of assessment.

- Effective reading professionals demonstrate a skilled use of assessment processes and results.

- Competent reading professionals are knowledgeable of standardized tests and their uses and limitations in the assessment process.

- Effective reading professionals are able to analyze data and communicate findings and implications to appropriate audiences.

Research and Supporting Literature

The content of this standard reflects the Standards 2010 Committee's interpretation of the professional literature in the area of teacher preparation in reading as related to issues of assessment. Some of the readings are foundational to education and teacher preparation generally, whereas others are specific to reading teacher preparation. Not exhaustive of this literature, the following list of readings represents the work of key theorists, researchers, and educators:

Afflerbach, P. (2007). *Understanding and using reading assessment, K–12*. Newark, DE: International Reading Association.

Bell, S.M., & McCallum, S. (2008). *Handbook of reading assessment*. Boston: Allyn & Bacon.

Fisher, D., & Ivey, G. (2006). Evaluating the interventions for struggling adolescent readers. *Journal of Adolescent & Adult Literacy*, 50(3), 180–189. doi:10.1598/JAAL.50.3.2

Invernizzi, M.A., Landrum, T.J., Howell, J.L., & Warley, H.P. (2005). Toward the peaceful coexistence of test developers, policymakers, and teachers in an era of accountability. *The Reading Teacher*, 58(7), 610–618. doi:10.1598/RT.58.7.2

Johnston, P., & Costello, P. (2005). Theory and research into practice: Principles for literacy assessment. *Reading Research Quarterly*, 40(2), 256–267. doi:10.1598/RRQ.40.2.6

Klauda, S.L., & Guthrie, J.T. (2008). Relationships of three components of reading fluency to reading comprehension. *Journal of Educational Psychology*, 100(2), 310–321. doi:10.1037/0022-0663.100.2.310

McAndrews, S.L. (2008). *Diagnostic literacy assessments and instructional strategies: A literacy specialist's resource*. Newark, DE: International Reading Association.

McKenna, M.C., & Walpole, S. (2005). How well does assessment inform our reading instruction? *The Reading Teacher*, 59(1), 84–86. doi:10.1598/RT.59.1.9

Shepard, L.A. (2004). The role of assessment in a learning culture. In R.B. Ruddell & N.J. Unrau (Eds.), *Theoretical models and processes of reading* (5th ed., pp. 1614–1635). Newark, DE: International Reading Association.

Taylor, B.M., Pearson, P.D., Clark, K., & Walpole, S. (2000). Effective schools and accomplished teachers: Lessons about primary-grade reading instruction in low-income schools. *The Elementary School Journal, 101*(2), 121–165. doi:10.1086/499662

Tierney, R.J., Moore, D.W., Valencia, S.W., & Johnston, P. (2000). How will literacy be assessed in the next millennium? *Reading Research Quarterly, 35*(2), 244–250. doi:10.1598/RRQ.35.2.3

Valencia, S.W., & Wixson, K.K. (2000). Policy-oriented research on literacy standards and assessment. In M.L. Kamil, P.B. Mosenthal, P.D. Pearson, & R. Barr (Eds.), *Handbook of reading research* (Vol. 3, pp. 909–935). Mahwah, NJ: Erlbaum.

Standard 4: Diversity

Candidates create and engage their students in literacy practices that develop awareness, understanding, respect, and a valuing of differences in our society.

The Diversity Standard focuses on the need to prepare teachers to build and engage their students in a curriculum that places value on the diversity that exists in our society, as featured in elements such as race, ethnicity, class, gender, religion, and language. This standard is grounded in a set of principles and understandings that reflect a vision for a democratic and just society and inform the effective preparation of reading professionals.

The following are the major assumptions of the Standards 2010 Committee for developing this standard and its elements:

- Diversity will be as much a reality in the future as it is in our lives today and has been in the lives of our predecessors.

- There is a tradition of "deficit" thinking and discourse in the context of diversity and schooling. As a society, we are not far removed from a time when *cultural deprivation* was an accepted term.

- Diversity is a potential source of strength of a society to be encouraged not discouraged. Diversity is the basis for adaptability to change, and change is the only certainty in the future.

- Creating a curriculum that values diversity requires that teacher educators and teachers step outside their personal experiences within a particular linguistic, ethnic, or cultural group to experience the offerings of other groups.

- The elements of diversity in a society cannot be isolated within that society and certainly not within an individual. The elements of diversity interact in the form of multiple identities that may move from the background into the foreground as a function of the context and the moment.

- There is a danger in overgeneralizing (i.e., stereotyping) characteristics to all members of a group.

- Language-minority students need appropriate and different language and literacy instruction if they are to be successful academically while they learn English.

- It is the responsibility of teachers and schools not only to prepare learners in ways that value their diversity but also to prepare those learners to engage in active citizenship to redress areas of inequity and privilege.

Research and Supporting Literature

The content of this standard reflects our interpretation of the professional literature in the area of teacher preparation in reading as related to issues of diversity. Some of these readings are foundational to education and teacher preparation generally, whereas others are specific to reading teacher preparation. Not exhaustive of this literature, the following list of readings represents the work of many key theorists, researchers, and educators:

Au, K.H., & Raphael, T.E. (2000). Equity and literacy in the next millennium. *Reading Research Quarterly, 35*(1), 170–188. doi:10.1598/RRQ.35.1.12

Delpit, L. (2006). *Other people's children: Cultural conflict in the classroom.* New York: New Press.

Gay, G. (2000). *Culturally responsive teaching: Theory, research, and practice.* New York: Teachers College Press.

Gollnick, D.M., & Chinn, P.C. (2008). *Multicultural education in a pluralistic society* (8th ed.). Boston: Allyn & Bacon.

González, N., Moll, L.C., & Amanti, C. (2005). *Funds of knowledge: Theorizing practices in households, communities, and classrooms.* Mahwah, NJ: Erlbaum.

Gunderson, L. (2007). *English-only instruction and immigrant students in secondary schools: A critical examination.* Mahwah, NJ: Erlbaum.

Ladson-Billings, G. (2001). *Crossing over to Canaan: The journey of new teachers in diverse classrooms.* San Francisco: Jossey-Bass.

Ladson-Billings, G. (2009). *The dreamkeepers: Successful teachers of African American children* (2nd ed.). San Francisco: Jossey-Bass.

Rogers, R., & Mosley, M. (2006). Racial literacy in a second-grade classroom: Critical race theory, whiteness studies, and literacy research. *Reading Research Quarterly, 41*(4), 462–495. doi:10.1598/RRQ.41.4.3

Smith, G.P. (1998). *Common sense about uncommon knowledge: The knowledge bases for diversity.* Washington, DC: American Association of Colleges for Teacher Education.

Thornton, H. (2006). Dispositions in action: Do dispositions make a difference in practice? *Teacher Education Quarterly, 33*(2), 53–68.

Valenzuela, A. (1999). *Subtractive schooling: U.S.-Mexican youth and the politics of caring.* Albany: State University of New York Press.

Standard 5: Literate Environment

Candidates create a literate environment that fosters reading and writing by integrating foundational knowledge, instructional practices, approaches and methods, curriculum materials, and the appropriate use of assessments.

The Literate Environment Standard focuses on the need for candidates to synthesize their foundational knowledge about content, pedagogy, the effective use of physical space, instructional materials and technology, and the impact of the social environment to create an environment that fosters and supports students' traditional print, digital, and online reading and writing achievement. This standard recognizes that candidates must create a literate environment that meets the diverse needs of students and facilitates connections across content areas as well as with the world outside the school.

The following are the major assumptions of the Standards 2010 Committee for developing this standard and its elements:

- An effective literate environment offers both visible and "invisible" support (i.e., psychological, social, emotional) to learners as they expand their literacies.

- The goal of the literate environment is to create a flexible border between the world outside the classroom and school to the world within (i.e., making the curriculum permeable to the social context). Learning should extend beyond the walls of the educational context to explore the potential for acts of literacy that affect the world outside.

- Learners require a literate environment that affords them the opportunity to engage in meaningful ways by providing time, accessibility, tools, choice, and support.

- Student learning is positively impacted by positive teacher dispositions, such as high expectations, a carefully crafted physical environment, and a safe, low-risk social environment.

- To meet the needs of learners, a coconstructed literate environment must continually change as interests and focal points for learning shift over time.

Research and Supporting Literature

The following are representative research and literature consulted by the Standards 2010 Committee in developing this standard:

Barr, R., & Dreeben, R. (1991). Grouping students for reading instruction. In R. Barr, M.L. Kamil, P. Mosenthal, & P.D. Pearson (Eds.), *Handbook of reading research* (Vol. 2, pp. 885–910). New York: Longman.

Castle, S., Deniz, C.B., & Tortora, M. (2005). Flexible grouping and student learning in a high-needs school. *Education and Urban Society, 37*(2), 139–150. doi:10.1177/0013124504270787

Dowhower, S.L., & Beagle, K.G. (1998). The print environment in kindergartens: A study of conventional and holistic teachers and their classrooms in three settings. *Reading Research and Instruction, 37*(3), 161–190.

Fractor, J.S., Woodruff, M.C., Martinez, M.G., & Teale, W.H. (1993). Let's not miss opportunities to promote voluntary reading: Classroom libraries in the elementary school. *The Reading Teacher, 46*(6), 476–484.

Guthrie, J.T., Wigfield, A., Humenick, N.M., Perencevich, K.C., Taboada, A., & Barbosa, P. (2006). Influences of stimulating tasks on reading motivation and comprehension. *The Journal of Educational Research, 99*(4), 232–246. doi:10.3200/JOER.99.4.232-246

Hadjioannou, X. (2007). Bringing the background to the foreground: What do classroom environments that support authentic discussions look like? *American Educational Research Journal, 44*(2), 370–399. doi:10.3102/0002831207302173

Hoffman, J.V., Sailors, M., Duffy, G.R., & Beretvas, S.N. (2004). The effective elementary classroom literacy environment: Examining the validity of the TEX-IN3 observation system. *Journal of Literacy Research, 36*(3), 303–334. doi:10.1207/s15548430jlr3603_3

Loughlin, C.E., & Ivener, B.L. (1987). *Literacy behaviors of kindergarten-primary children in high stimulus-level literacy environments.* Albuquerque: University of New Mexico and Albuquerque Public Schools. (ERIC Document Reproduction Service No. ED354077)

McGill-Franzen, A., Allington, R.L., Yokoi, L., & Brooks, G. (1999). Putting books in the classroom seems necessary but not sufficient. *The Journal of Educational Research, 93*(2), 67–74. doi:10.1080/00220679909597631

Morrow, L.M. (1991). Relationships among physical designs of play centers, teachers' emphasis on literacy in play, and children's literacy behaviors during play. In J. Zutell & S. McCormick (Eds.), *Fortieth yearbook of the National Reading Conference: Learner factors/teacher factors: Issues in literacy research and instruction* (pp. 127–140). Chicago: National Reading Conference.

Proctor, C.P., Dalton, B., & Grisham, D.L. (2007). Scaffolding English language learners and struggling readers in a universal literacy environment with embedded strategy instruction and vocabulary support. *Journal of Literacy Research, 39*(1), 71–93. doi:10.1080/10862960709336758

Schulz, M.M., & Kantor, R. (2005). Understanding the home-school interface in a culturally diverse family. *Literacy Teaching and Learning, 10*(1), 59–79.

Snyder, I., Angus, L., & Sutherland-Smith, W. (2002). Building equitable literate futures: Home and school computer-mediated literacy practices and disadvantages. *Cambridge Journal of Education, 32*(3), 367–383. doi:10.1080/0305764022000024212

Taylor, N.E., Blum, I.H., & Logsdon, D.M. (1986). The development of written language awareness: Environmental aspects and program characteristics. *Reading Research Quarterly, 21*(2), 132–149. doi:10.2307/747841

Wolfersberger, M.E., Reutzel, D.R., Sudweeks, R., & Fawson, P.C. (2004). Developing and validating the classroom literacy environmental profile (CLEP): A tool for examining the "print richness" of early childhood and elementary classrooms. *Journal of Literacy Research, 36*(2), 211–272. doi:10.1207/s15548430jlr3602_4

Standard 6: Professional Learning and Leadership

Candidates recognize the importance of, demonstrate, and facilitate professional learning and leadership as a career-long effort and responsibility.

The Professional Learning and Leadership Standard is based on a commitment by all reading professionals to lifelong learning. Professionals learn in many different ways, for example, individual learning through activities such as reading, pursuing advanced degrees, and attending professional meetings. The elements featured in this standard include an emphasis on positive dispositions, individual and collaborative learning, the ability to design and evaluate professional learning experiences, the importance of advocacy, and a need for knowledge about adult learning and school leadership. Also, learning is often collaborative and occurs in the workplace through grade-level meetings, academic team meetings, workshops, study groups, and so forth.

The following are the major assumptions of the Standards 2010 Committee for developing this standard and its elements:

- Effective professional learning is evidence based in ways that reflect both competent and critical use of relevant research and is thoughtfully planned, ongoing, differentiated, and embedded in the work of all faculty members.

- Effective professional learning is inclusive and collaborative across parents or guardians, the community, and all school staff, including education support personnel, classroom teachers, specialized personnel, supervisors, and administrators.

- Effective professional learning is focused on content determined by careful consideration and assessment of the needs of students, teachers, parents or guardians, and the larger community of stakeholders.

- Effective professional learning is supportive of the need for instruction that is responsive to the range of diversity.

- Effective professional learning is grounded in research related to adult learning and organizational change as well as research on reading acquisition, development, assessment, and instruction.

- Effective professional learning in schools requires collaboration, is job embedded, builds trust, and empowers teachers, and those who lead such efforts must have effective interpersonal, leadership, and communication skills.

Research and Supporting Literature

The following are representative research and literature consulted by the Standards 2010 Committee in developing this standard:

Allington, R.L., & Walmsley, S.A. (Eds.). (1995). *No quick fix: Rethinking literacy programs in America's elementary schools*. New York: Teachers College Press; Newark, DE: International Reading Association.

Bean, R.M. (2009). *The reading specialist: Leadership for the classroom, school, and community* (2nd ed.). New York: Guilford.

Bean, R.M., Swan, A.L., & Knaub, R. (2003). Reading specialists in schools with exemplary reading programs: Functional, versatile, and prepared. *The Reading Teacher*, *56*(5), 446–455.

Darling-Hammond, L. (1999). *Teacher quality and student achievement: A review of state policy evidence*. Seattle, WA: Center for the Study of Teaching and Policy.

Desimone, L.M., Smith, T.M., & Ueno, K. (2006). Are teachers who need sustained, content-focused professional development getting it? An administrator's dilemma. *Educational Administration Quarterly*, *42*(2), 179–215. doi:10.1177/0013161X04273848

Dozier, C. (2006). *Responsive literacy coaching: Tools for creating and sustaining purposeful change*. Portland, ME: Stenhouse.

Duffy, G.G. (2004). Teachers who improve reading achievement: What research says about what they do and how to develop them. In D.S. Strickland & M.L. Kamil (Eds.), *Improving reading achievement through professional development* (pp. 3–22). Norwood, MA: Christopher-Gordon.

Garet, M.S., Porter, A.C., Desimone, L., Birman, B.F., & Yoon, K.S. (2001). What makes professional development effective? Results from a national sample of teachers. *American Educational Research Journal*, *38*(4), 915–945. doi:10.3102/00028312038004915

Lambert, L. (2003). *Leadership capacity for lasting school improvement*. Alexandria, VA: Association for Supervision and Curriculum Development.

Lyons, C.A., & Pinnell, G.S. (2001). *Systems for change in literacy education: A guide to professional development*. Portsmouth, NH: Heinemann.

Pritchard, R.J., & Marshall, J.C. (2002). Professional development in 'healthy' vs. 'unhealthy' districts: Top 10 characteristics based on research. *School Leadership & Management*, *22*(2), 113–141. doi:10.1080/1363243022000007719

Snow, C.E., Griffin, P., & Burns, M.S. (Eds.). (2005). *Knowledge to support the teaching of reading: Preparing teachers for a changing world*. San Francisco: Jossey-Bass.

Strickland, D.S., & Kamil, M.L. (Eds.). (2004). *Improving reading achievement through professional development*. Norwood, MA: Christopher-Gordon.

Sturtevant, E.G. (2003). *The literacy coach: A key to improving teaching and learning in secondary schools*. Washington, DC: Alliance for Excellent Education.

Thornton, H. (2006). Dispositions in action: Do dispositions make a difference in practice? *Teacher Education Quarterly, 33*(2), 53–68.

Vogt, M., & Shearer, B.A. (2007). *Reading specialists and literacy coaches in the real world* (2nd ed.). Boston: Pearson.

Walpole, S., & McKenna, M.C. (2004). *The literacy coach's handbook: A guide to research-based practice*. New York: Guilford.

Wepner, S.B., & Strickland, D.S. (Eds.). (2008). *The administration and supervision of reading programs* (4th ed.). New York: Teachers College Press.

Matrixes of All Standards Across the Roles

On the following pages of this section, the Standards and their elements are presented for each of the specialized roles that have some responsibility for reading instruction in schools. Also, recommendations are made of specific evidence that can be used to demonstrate competence of the elements for each role.

Standard 1: Foundational Knowledge

Element	Evidence that demonstrates competence may include, but is not limited to, the following:		
Candidates...	Education Support Personnel Candidates	Pre-K and Elementary Classroom Teacher Candidates	Middle and High School Content Classroom Teacher Candidates
1.1: Understand major theories and empirical research that describe the cognitive, linguistic, motivational, and sociocultural foundations of reading and writing development, processes, and components, including word recognition, language comprehension, strategic knowledge, and reading–writing connections.	• Identify examples of reading instruction for developing word recognition, language comprehension, strategic knowledge, and reading–writing connections. • Identify conditions that support individual motivation to read and write (e.g., access to print, choice, challenge, interests, and family and community knowledge) as factors that enhance literacy learning for all.	• Recognize major theories of reading and writing processes and development, including first and second literacy acquisition and the role of native language in learning to read and write in a second language. • Explain language and reading development across elementary years (e.g., word recognition, language comprehension, strategic knowledge, and reading–writing connections) using supporting evidence from theory and research. • Demonstrate knowledge about transfer of skills from the primary or home language (L1) to English (L2) as it affects literacy learning across these components. • Explain the research and theory about effective learning environments that support individual motivation to read and write (e.g., choice, challenge, interests, and access to traditional print, digital, and online resources).	• Recognize major theories and research evidence of reading and writing processes and development in adolescence, including first and second literacy acquisition and the role of native language in learning to read and write in a second language. • Identify and explain the specific reading and writing expectations of their content areas as described in national and state standards. • Explain the research and theory of learning environments that support individual motivation to read and write. • Value the scholarship of the reading profession and seek to understand the theoretical knowledge base in relation to their disciplinary areas. • Understand the process of identifying and differentiating the range of literacy needs of adolescent readers.	
1.2: Understand the historically shared knowledge of the profession and changes over time in the perceptions of reading and writing development, processes, and components.	Not applicable	• Identify major milestones in reading scholarship and interpret them in light of the current social context.	Not applicable	
1.3: Understand the role of professional judgment and practical knowledge for improving all students' reading development and achievement.	• Show fair-mindeness, empathy, and ethical behavior when teaching students and working with other professionals.	• Show fair-mindeness, empathy, and ethical behavior in literacy instruction and when working with other professionals. • Use multiple sources of information to guide instructional planning to improve reading achievement of all students.	• Show fair-mindeness, empathy, and ethical behavior when teaching students and working with other professionals. • Use multiple sources of information to guide instructional planning to improve reading achievement of all students.	

Middle and High School Reading Classroom Teacher Candidates	Reading Specialist/Literacy Coach Candidates	Teacher Educator Candidates	Administrator Candidates
• Read the scholarship of the reading profession and recognize the theoretical knowledge base about the reading and writing of adolescents. • Explain major theories of reading and writing processes and development in adolescents using supporting research evidence, including the relationship between culture and the native language of English learners as a support system in their learning to read and write in English. • Explain language and reading development during adolescence (e.g., word recognition, language comprehension, strategic knowledge, and reading–writing connections) with supporting evidence from theory and research. • Explain the research and theory of learning environments that support individual motivation to read and write.	• Interpret major theories of reading and writing processes and development to understand the needs of all readers in diverse contexts. • Analyze classroom environment quality for fostering individual motivation to read and write (e.g., access to print, choice, challenge, and interests). • Demonstrate a critical stance toward the scholarship of the profession. • Read and understand the literature and research about factors that contribute to reading success (e.g., social, cognitive, and physical). • Inform other educators about major theories of reading and writing processes, components, and development with supporting research evidence, including information about the relationship between the culture and native language of English learners as a support system in their learning to read and write in English.	• Critique major theories of reading and writing processes, components, and development across the life span using research evidence. • Analyze research evidence about language and reading development in all areas, including knowledge about transfer of skills from the primary or home language (L1) to English (L2) as it affects literacy learning for English learners across those components. • Create environments in the university classroom that foster individual motivation to read and write (e.g., access to print, choice, challenge, and interests) and teach teachers how to create such environments. • Evaluate knowledge claims of reading research, critique research findings, and generate alternative hypotheses.	• Recognize major theories and research evidence related to reading and writing development and instruction. • Identify specific reading and writing expectations for pre-K–12 students as described in national and state standards. • Plan for environments that support individual motivation to read and write (e.g., access to print, choice, challenge, and interests). • Value the scholarship of the reading profession and seek to understand the theoretical knowledge base in relation to their administrative charges.
• Identify major milestones in reading scholarship and interpret them in light of the current social context.	• Interpret and summarize historically shared knowledge (e.g., instructional strategies and theories) that addresses the needs of all readers. • Inform educators and others about the historically shared knowledge base in reading and writing and its role in reading education.	• Analyze historically shared knowledge in reading and writing scholarship and explain its role in an evolving professional knowledge base. • Reevaluate the relevance of historically shared knowledge for meeting traditional print, digital, and online reading education goals.	• Identify evidence-based instructional approaches, techniques, and procedures relevant to the reading and writing demands of pre-K–12 instruction. • Critically examine practices that contribute to applied knowledge of reading education.
• Show fair-mindedness, empathy, and ethical behavior when teaching students and working with other professionals. • Use multiple sources of information to guide instructional planning to improve reading achievement of all students.	• Model fair-mindedness, empathy, and ethical behavior when teaching students and working with other professionals. • Communicate the importance of fair-mindedness, empathy, and ethical behavior in literacy instruction and professional behavior.	• Communicate the importance of fair-mindedness, empathy, and ethical behavior in professional activity.	• Encourage reading professionals to show fair-mindedness, empathy, and ethical behavior when teaching students and working with other professionals. • Model such behaviors when working with professional staff.

Standard 2: Curriculum and Instruction

Element	Evidence that demonstrates competence may include, but is not limited to, the following:		
Candidates...	Education Support Personnel Candidates	Pre-K and Elementary Classroom Teacher Candidates	Middle and High School Content Classroom Teacher Candidates
2.1: Use foundational knowledge to design or implement an integrated, comprehensive, and balanced curriculum.	• Implement lessons that are part of the reading and writing curriculum with teacher guidance and supervision.	• Explain how the reading and writing curriculum is related to local, state, national and professional standards. • Implement the curriculum based on students' prior knowledge, world experiences, and interests. • Evaluate the curriculum to ensure that instructional goals and objectives are met. • Plan with other teachers and support personnel in designing, adjusting, and modifying the curriculum to meet students' needs in traditional print, digital, and online contexts.	• Explain how reading and writing relate to their content areas and to local, state, national and professional standards. • Implement the curriculum based on students' prior knowledge, world experiences, and interests. • Evaluate the curriculum to ensure that instructional goals and objectives meet the reading and writing demands of the content areas. • Work with other teachers and support personnel to design, adjust, and modify the curriculum to meet students' literacy needs. • Support students as agents of their own learning and critical consumers of the discipline.
2.2: Use appropriate and varied instructional approaches, including those that develop word recognition, language comprehension, strategic knowledge, and reading–writing connections.	• Use a wide range of instructional approaches selected and supervised by the teacher.	• Select and implement instructional approaches based on evidence-based rationale, student needs, and purposes for instruction. • Differentiate instructional approaches to meet students' reading and writing needs. • Implement and evaluate instruction in each of the following areas: concepts of print, phonemic awareness, phonics, vocabulary, comprehension, fluency, critical thinking, motivation, and writing. • Incorporate traditional print, digital, and online resources as instructional tools to enhance student learning. • As needed, adapt instructional approaches and materials to meet the language-proficiency needs of English learners.	• Select and implement content area reading and writing instructional approaches based on evidence-based rationale, student needs, and purposes for instruction. • Differentiate instructional approaches to meet students' reading and writing needs in the content areas. • Implement and evaluate content area instruction in each of the following areas: vocabulary meaning, comprehension, writing, motivation, and critical thinking. • Incorporate traditional print, digital, and online resources as instructional tools to enhance student learning. • As needed, adapt instructional approaches and materials to meet the language-proficiency needs of English learners.
2.3: Use a wide range of texts (e.g., narrative, expository, and poetry) from traditional print, digital, and online resources.	• With guidance from teachers, select and use a wide range of materials.	• Guided by evidence-based rationale, select and use quality traditional print, digital, and online resources. • Build an accessible, multilevel, and diverse classroom library that contains traditional print, digital, and online classroom materials.	• Demonstrate knowledge about various materials and their uses. • Guided by evidence-based rationale, select and use quality traditional print, digital, and online resources. • Build an accessible, multilevel, and diverse classroom library for their content areas that contains traditional print, digital, and online resources.

Middle and High School Reading Classroom Teacher Candidates	Reading Specialist/Literacy Coach Candidates	Teacher Educator Candidates	Administrator Candidates
• Explain how reading and writing relates to their content area and the local, state, national, and professional standards. • Implement the curriculum based on students' prior knowledge, world experiences, and interests. • Evaluate the curriculum to ensure that instructional goals and objectives are met. • Work with the team or department to help ensure interdisciplinary connections in traditional print, digital, and online contexts.	• Demonstrate an understanding of the research and literature that undergirds the reading and writing curriculum and instruction for all pre-K–12 students. • Develop and implement the curriculum to meet the specific needs of students who struggle with reading. • Support teachers and other personnel in the design, implementation, and evaluation of the reading and writing curriculum for all students. • Work with teachers and other personnel in developing a literacy curriculum that has vertical and horizontal alignment across pre-K–12.	• Demonstrate knowledge of and evaluate the pre-K–12 reading and writing curriculum. • Convey knowledge and understanding of the curriculum to reading professionals. • Provide opportunities for reading professionals to develop an integrated, comprehensive, and balanced curriculum.	• Monitor instruction to determine that local, state, and national standards are met. • Provide opportunities for review and alignment of the curriculum with local, state, and national standards.
• Select and implement reading and writing approaches that are evidence based and meet student needs. • Differentiate instructional approaches to meet students' reading and writing needs in the content areas. • Implement and evaluate content area instruction in each of the following elements: vocabulary meaning, comprehension, writing, motivation, and critical thinking. • Incorporate traditional print, digital, and online resources as instructional tools to enhance student learning. • As needed, adapt instructional approaches and materials to meet the language-proficiency needs of English learners.	• Use instructional approaches supported by literature and research for the following areas: concepts of print, phonemic awareness, phonics, vocabulary, comprehension, fluency, critical thinking, motivation, and writing. • Provide appropriate in-depth instruction for all readers and writers, especially those who struggle with reading and writing. • Support classroom teachers and education support personnel to implement instructional approaches for all students. • As needed, adapt instructional materials and approaches to meet the language-proficiency needs of English learners and students who struggle to learn to read and write.	• Provide opportunities for preservice teachers and other reading professionals to understand conceptual underpinnings and evidence-based rationales of instructional approaches. • Provide opportunities for preservice teachers and other reading professionals to select, implement, and evaluate instructional approaches based on knowledge of students' needs and interests, and theory-based knowledge.	• Provide ongoing, integrated professional development opportunities that allow the demonstration and modeling of evidence-based approaches. • Provide opportunities for teachers' self-reflection and interaction with peers. • Provide professional materials and encourage study/discussion groups.
• Demonstrate knowledge about various materials, including those specifically for adolescent learners, and their uses. • Guided by evidence-based rationale, select and use traditional print, digital, and online resources. • Build an accessible, multilevel, and diverse classroom library that contains traditional print, digital, and online resources.	• Demonstrate knowledge of and a critical stance toward a wide variety of quality traditional print, digital, and online resources. • Support classroom teachers in building and using a quality, accessible classroom library and materials collection that meets the specific needs and abilities of all learners. • Lead collaborative school efforts to evaluate, select, and use a variety of instructional materials to meet the specific needs and abilities of all learners.	• Provide opportunities for preservice teachers and other reading professionals to review and critique a wide variety of quality traditional print, digital, and online resources. • Provide opportunities for preservice teachers and other reading professionals to establish criteria for selecting quality traditional print, digital, and online resources for all students, including English learners.	• Demonstrate a critical stance toward instructional materials used for reading and writing instruction. • Provide opportunities for demonstrations, evaluations, and usage of a wide range of instructional materials that support student learning.

Standard 3: Assessment and Evaluation

Element	Evidence that demonstrates competence may include, but is not limited to, the following:		
Candidates...	Education Support Personnel Candidates	Pre-K and Elementary Classroom Teacher Candidates	Middle and High School Content Classroom Teacher Candidates
3.1: Understand types of assessments and their purposes, strengths, and limitations.	• Demonstrate an understanding of established purposes for assessing student performance.	• Demonstrate an understanding of established purposes for assessing student performance, including tools for screening, diagnosis, progress monitoring, and measuring outcomes. • Describe strengths and limitations of a range of assessment tools and their appropriate uses. • Recognize the basic technical adequacy of assessments (e.g., reliability, content, and construct validity). • Explain district and state assessment frameworks, proficiency standards, and student benchmarks.	• Demonstrate an understanding of reading and writing elements of content area assessments and their purposes in assessing student performance. • Describe the strengths and limitations of a range of assessment tools and their appropriate uses. • Recognize the basic technical adequacy of assessments (e.g., reliability, content, and construct validity). • Explain district and state assessment frameworks, proficiency standards, and student benchmarks.
3.2: Select, develop, administer, and interpret assessments, both traditional print and electronic, for specific purposes.	• Administer assessments under the direction of certified personnel.	• Select or develop appropriate assessment tools to monitor student progress and to analyze instructional effectiveness. • Administer classroom and school-based assessments using consistent, fair, and equitable assessment procedures. • Interpret and use assessment data to analyze individual, group, and classroom performance and progress. • Collaborate with other teachers and with support personnel to discuss interpretation of assessment data and their uses in responding to student needs and strengths.	• Select or develop assessment tools to analyze instructional effectiveness within the content areas. • Administer classroom and school-based assessments using consistent, fair, and equitable assessment procedures. • Interpret and use assessment data to analyze individual, group, and classroom performance and progress. • Collaborate with other teachers and with support personnel to discuss interpretation of assessment data and their uses in responding to student needs and strengths.
3.3: Use assessment information to plan and evaluate instruction.	• Support teachers in data collection and record keeping.	• Use assessment data to plan instruction systematically and to select appropriate traditional print, digital, and online reading resources. • Use assessment data to evaluate students' responses to instruction and to develop relevant next steps for teaching. • Interpret patterns in classroom and individual students' data. • Collaborate with other reading professionals to modify instruction and to plan and evaluate interventions based on assessment data.	• Analyze and use assessment data to plan and adjust instruction systematically and to select appropriate reading materials for use in the content areas. • Analyze and use assessment data to evaluate students' responses to instruction and to develop relevant next steps for teaching. • Identify and interpret patterns in classroom and individuals' student data. • Collaborate with reading teachers to identify relevant reading and writing strategies and skills for use in the specific content areas or disciplines.

Middle and High School Reading Classroom Teacher Candidates	Reading Specialist/Literacy Coach Candidates	Teacher Educator Candidates	Administrator Candidates
• Demonstrate an understanding of established purposes for assessing student performance, including tools for screening, diagnosis, progress monitoring, and measuring outcomes. • Describe the strengths and limitations of a range of assessment tools and their appropriate uses. • Recognize the basic technical adequacy of assessments (e.g., reliability, content, and construct validity). • Explain district and state assessment frameworks, proficiency standards, and student benchmarks.	• Demonstrate an understanding of the literature and research related to assessments and their uses and misuses. • Demonstrate an understanding of established purposes for assessing the performance of all readers, including tools for screening, diagnosis, progress monitoring, and measuring outcomes. • Recognize the basic technical adequacy of assessments (e.g., reliability, content, and construct validity). • Explain district and state assessment frameworks, proficiency standards, and student benchmarks.	• Prepare preservice teachers and other reading professionals to select, analyze, and use assessment tools based on established purposes. • Analyze and critique a range of assessment tools based on established purposes. • Contribute to the scholarly dialogue about assessment. • Read and understand the literature and research related to assessments and their uses and misuses.	• Demonstrate an understanding of the literature and research related to assessments and their uses and misuses. • Explain district and state assessment frameworks, proficiency standards, and student benchmarks. • Explain large-scale assessment designs, state and district assessment frameworks, proficiency standards, and benchmarks.
• Select or develop appropriate assessment tools to monitor student progress and to analyze instructional effectiveness. • Administer classroom and school-based assessments using consistent, fair, and equitable assessment procedures. • Recommend and administer assessments for students in need of reading and writing assistance. • Interpret and use assessment data to analyze individual, group, and classroom performance and progress within and across content areas and disciplines. • Collaborate with content teachers to monitor student progress and to analyze instructional effectiveness.	• Administer and interpret appropriate assessments for students, especially those who struggle with reading and writing. • Collaborate with and provide support to all teachers in the analysis of data, using the assessment results of all students. • Lead schoolwide or larger scale analyses to select assessment tools that provide a systemic framework for assessing the reading, writing, and language growth of all students.	• Prepare preservice teachers and other reading professionals to administer and interpret assessments for selected purposes. • Analyze and critique a range of diagnostic assessment tools for students in need of reading and writing assistance.	• Provide time and fiscal resources to facilitate assessment. • Support the development of sound assessment design across classrooms.
• Use assessment data to plan instruction systematically and to select appropriate traditional print, digital, and online reading resources. • Use assessment data to evaluate students' responses to instruction and to develop relevant next steps for teaching. • Identify and interpret patterns in classroom and individual students' data. • Collaborate with content area teachers to use assessment data to modify instruction, evaluate the effectiveness of instruction, and plan content literacy initiatives.	• Use multiple data sources to analyze individual readers' performance and to plan instruction and intervention. • Analyze and use assessment data to examine the effectiveness of specific intervention practices and students' responses to instruction. • Lead teachers in analyzing and using classroom, individual, grade-level, or schoolwide assessment data to make instructional decisions. • Plan and evaluate professional development initiatives using assessment data.	• Prepare preservice teachers and other reading professionals to examine the role of assessment in the delivery of effective reading instruction. • Prepare preservice teachers and other reading professionals to adjust instruction based on ongoing assessment.	• Use student data to facilitate curricular, grouping, and literacy staffing pattern decisions within schools, across schools, and within the district.

(continued)

Standard 3: Assessment and Evaluation *(continued)*

Element	Evidence that demonstrates competence may include, but is not limited to, the following:		
Candidates...	Education Support Personnel Candidates	Pre-K and Elementary Classroom Teacher Candidates	Middle and High School Content Classroom Teacher Candidates
3.4: Communicate assessment results and implications to a variety of audiences.	• Understand the importance of student confidentiality and acknowledge the role of certified personnel as communicators of assessment results.	• Communicate assessment purposes and a summary of results to appropriate audiences (i.e., student, parents or guardians, colleagues, and administrators). • Use assessment data and student work samples to discuss relevant implications and goals for reading and writing instruction.	• Communicate assessment purposes and a summary of results to appropriate audiences (i.e., student, parents or guardians, colleagues, and administrators). • Use assessment data and student work samples to discuss implications for the content area or literacy instruction (e.g., highlight differences in student work samples across a content area).

Standard 4: Diversity

Element	Evidence that demonstrates competence may include, but is not limited to, the following:		
Candidates...	Education Support Personnel Candidates	Pre-K and Elementary Classroom Teacher Candidates	Middle and High School Content Classroom Teacher Candidates
4.1: Recognize, understand, and value the forms of diversity that exist in society and their importance in learning to read and write.	• Recognize the forms of diversity in their own lives and understand how these may limit or enable their reading and writing. • Demonstrate an understanding of the forms of diversity that exist in society, with a particular focus on individual and group differences that have been used to marginalize some and privilege others. • Value diversity as a resource in a functioning democratic society.	• Demonstrate an understanding of the ways in which diversity can be used to strengthen a literate society, making it more productive, more adaptable to change, and more equitable. • Demonstrate an understanding of the impact of urban, suburban, and rural environments on local culture, language, and learning to read and write. • Demonstrate an understanding of the ways in which the various forms of diversity interact with reading and writing development. • Demonstrate an understanding of the relationship between first- and second-language acquisition and literacy development.	• Demonstrate an understanding of the ways in which diversity can be used to strengthen a literate society, making it more productive, more adaptable to change, and more equitable. • Demonstrate an understanding of the impact of urban, suburban, and rural environments on local culture, language, and learning to read and write. • Demonstrate an understanding of the ways in which various forms of diversity interact with adolescent literacy development and content area learning. • Demonstrate an understanding of the relationship between first- and second-language acquisition and literacy development.

Middle and High School Reading Classroom Teacher Candidates	Reading Specialist/Literacy Coach Candidates	Teacher Educator Candidates	Administrator Candidates
• Communicate assessment purposes and discuss results with appropriate audiences (i.e., student, parents or guardians, colleagues, and administrators). • Use assessment data and student work samples to discuss implications for reading and writing instruction (e.g., highlight differences in student work samples across the content areas).	• Analyze and report assessment results to a variety of appropriate audiences for relevant implications, instructional purposes, and accountability. • Demonstrate the ability to communicate results of assessments to various audiences.	• Prepare and coach preservice teachers and other reading professionals to communicate assessment results to various audiences in ways that lead to improved instruction.	• Analyze and communicate local, state, and federal assessment results to internal staff and external partners (e.g., community members, policymakers, and other stakeholders). • Analyze and communicate literacy performance goals as identified in federal and state laws and the implications of those goals on literacy curriculum, instruction, and assessment.

Middle and High School Reading Classroom Teacher Candidates	Reading Specialist/Literacy Coach Candidates	Teacher Educator Candidates	Administrator Candidates
• Demonstrate an understanding of the ways in which diversity can be used to strengthen a literate society, making it more productive, more adaptable to change, and more equitable. • Demonstrate an understanding of the impact of urban, suburban, and rural environments on local culture, language, and learning to read and write. • Demonstrate an understanding of the ways in which diversity influences adolescent literacy development. • Demonstrate an understanding of the relationship between first- and second-language acquisition and literacy development.	• Demonstrate an understanding of the ways in which diversity influences the reading and writing development of all students, especially those who struggle with reading and writing. • Assist teachers in developing reading and writing instruction that is responsive to diversity. • Assist teachers in understanding the relationship between first- and second-language acquisition and literacy development. • Engage the school community in conversations about research on diversity and how diversity impacts reading and writing development.	• Demonstrate an understanding of current theoretical perspectives and empirical evidence related to diversity and reading and writing development. • Prepare preservice teachers and other reading professionals to understand the relationship between first- and second-language acquisition and literacy development.	• Examine, evaluate, and articulate how students' diversity informs pedagogy, the selection of curricula, and professional development practices. • Support and collaborate with teachers, parents and guardians, and community members to provide experiences that are responsive to students' diverse needs. • Plan for and sustain school cultures that are supportive of the diversity that exists among teachers and students.

(continued)

Standard 4: Diversity *(continued)*

Element	Evidence that demonstrates competence may include, but is not limited to, the following:		
Candidates...	Education Support Personnel Candidates	Pre-K and Elementary Classroom Teacher Candidates	Middle and High School Content Classroom Teacher Candidates
4.2: Use a literacy curriculum and engage in instructional practices that positively impact students' knowledge, beliefs, and engagement with the features of diversity.	• Describe specific aspects of school and community experiences that can be used to reveal students' diversity and engage them in learning. • Assist in instructional practices that are linked to students' diversity and which also acquaint them with others' traditions and diversity. • Assist in instructional practices that engage students as agents of their own learning.	• Assess the various forms of diversity that exist in students as well as in the surrounding community. • Provide differentiated instruction and instructional materials, including traditional print, digital, and online resources, that capitalize on diversity. • Provide instruction and instructional materials that are linked to students' backgrounds and facilitate a learning environment in which differences and commonalities are valued (e.g., use literature that reflects the experiences of marginalized groups and the strategies they use to overcome challenges). • Provide instruction and instructional formats that engage students as agents of their own learning.	• Assess the various forms of diversity that exist in students as well as in the surrounding community. • Provide differentiated instruction and instructional materials, including traditional print, digital, and online resources, that capitalize on diversity. • Provide instructional formats that engage students as agents of their own learning.
4.3: Develop and implement strategies to advocate for equity.	• Use their literacy skills to assist communities that are experiencing discrimination to overcome it (e.g., volunteer in the development of or teach in an adult literacy or English as a second language program).	• Provide students with linguistic, academic, and cultural experiences that link their communities with the school. • Advocate for change in societal practices and institutional structures that are inherently biased or prejudiced against certain groups. • Demonstrate how issues of inequity and opportunities for social justice activism and resiliency can be incorporated into the literacy curriculum.	• Provide students with linguistic, academic, and cultural experiences that link their backgrounds with content area learning. • Advocate for change in societal practices and institutional structures that are inherently biased or prejudiced against certain groups. • Demonstrate how issues of inequity and opportunities for social justice activism and resiliency in students' communities can be incorporated into the content areas and literacy curriculum.

Middle and High School Reading Classroom Teacher Candidates	Reading Specialist/Literacy Coach Candidates	Teacher Educator Candidates	Administrator Candidates
• Assess the various forms of diversity that exist in students as well as in the surrounding community. • Provide differentiated instruction and instructional materials, including traditional print, digital, and online resources, that capitalize on diversity. • Provide instructional formats that engage students as agents of their own learning.	• Provide differentiated instruction and instructional materials, including traditional print, digital, and online resources, that capitalize on diversity. • Support classroom teachers in providing differentiated instruction and developing students as agents of their own literacy learning. • Support and lead other educators to recognize their own cultures in order to teach in ways that are responsive to students' diverse backgrounds. • Collaborate with others to build strong home-to-school and school-to-home literacy connections. • Provide support and leadership to educators, parents and guardians, students, and other members of the school community in valuing the contributions of diverse people and traditions to literacy learning.	• Engage preservice teachers and other reading professionals in multiple experiences and settings to strengthen their understandings about the ways that multiple identities of students intersect with curriculum orientations, literacy instruction, and student agency. • Collaborate with preservice teachers and other reading professionals to identify and advocate for forms of pedagogy, curriculum orientations, and professional development practices that focus on students' diversity. • Provide opportunities for preservice teachers and other reading professionals to reflect on and evaluate literacy-related experiences aimed at providing responsive instruction that honors students' diversity.	• Examine, evaluate, and articulate how instructional programs, curricular materials, and assessment practices impact the literacy outcomes of diverse students. • Identify human and material resources to effectively shape learning environments that are responsive to the various features of student diversity.
• Provide students with linguistic, academic, and cultural experiences that link their communities with the school. • Advocate for change in societal practices and institutional structures that are inherently biased or prejudiced against certain groups. • Demonstrate how issues of inequity and opportunities for social justice activism and resiliency can be incorporated into the literacy curriculum.	• Provide students with linguistic, academic, and cultural experiences that link their communities with the school. • Advocate for change in societal practices and institutional structures that are inherently biased or prejudiced against certain groups. • Demonstrate how issues of inequity and opportunities for social justice activism and resiliency can be incorporated into the literacy curriculum. • Collaborate with teachers, parents and guardians, and administrators to implement policies and instructional practices that promote equity and draw connections between home and community literacy and school literacy.	• Prepare, coach, and collaborate with preservice teachers and other reading professionals to respond to literacy practices, both in and out of school, that are inequitable and unfair and replace them with practices that are equitable and fair. • Provide and promote experiences for reading professionals that reflect and nurture the ideas of tolerance and equity.	• Ensure that school contexts, structures, and teachers' professional practices are supportive of, responsive to, and respectful of teachers', students', and families' diversity. • Collaborate with all stakeholders to mobilize efforts to be responsive to students' diversity.

Standard 5: Literate Environment

Element	Evidence that demonstrates competence may include, but is not limited to, the following:		
Candidates...	Education Support Personnel Candidates	Pre-K and Elementary Classroom Teacher Candidates	Middle and High School Content Classroom Teacher Candidates
5.1: Design the physical environment to optimize students' use of traditional print, digital, and online resources in reading and writing instruction.	• Assist classroom teachers in developing and maintaining physical arrangements of traditional print, digital, and online resources that facilitate reading and writing instruction.	• Arrange their classrooms to provide easy access to books, other instructional materials, and specific areas designed for a variety of individual, small-group, and whole-class activities. • Modify the arrangements to accommodate students' changing needs.	• Arrange their classrooms to provide easy access to books, other instructional materials, and specific areas designed for a variety of individual, small-group, and whole-class activities. • Modify the arrangements to accommodate students' changing needs.
5.2: Design a social environment that is low risk and includes choice, motivation, and scaffolded support to optimize students' opportunities for learning to read and write.	• Assist classroom teachers in creating and maintaining positive social environments.	• Demonstrate a respectful attitude toward all learners and understand the roles of choice, motivation, and scaffolded support in creating low-risk and positive social environments. • Model and teach students routines for establishing and maintaining positive social environments (e.g., appropriate ways to interact with each other and adults). • Create supportive environments where English learners are encouraged and given many opportunities to use English.	• Demonstrate a respectful attitude toward all learners and understand the roles of choice, motivation, and scaffolded support in creating low-risk and positive social environments. • Model and teach students appropriate ways to interact with each other and adults. • Create supportive environments where English learners are encouraged and given many opportunities to use English.
5.3: Use routines to support reading and writing instruction (e.g., time allocation, transitions from one activity to another, discussions, and peer feedback).	• Understand how and why classroom teachers use specific routines. • Assist classroom teachers in creating and maintaining those routines.	• Understand the role of routines in creating and maintaining positive learning environments for reading and writing instruction using traditional print, digital, and online resources. • Create and use routines to support instructional and social goals (e.g., regular steps for sharing and responding to stories, formats for reporting, and efficient transitions among activities, spaces, and online resources).	• Understand the role of routines in creating and maintaining positive learning environments for content area learning using traditional print, digital, and online resources. • Create and use routines to support instructional and social goals (e.g., regular steps for sharing and responding to stories, formats for reporting, and efficient transitions among activities, spaces, and online resources).
5.4: Use a variety of classroom configurations (i.e., whole class, small group, and individual) to differentiate instruction.	• Use a variety of instructional grouping options selected by and supervised by the classroom teachers. • In consultation with the teachers, adjust instructional groupings to ensure that the diverse needs of learners are being met.	• Use evidence-based rationale to make and monitor flexible instructional grouping options for students. • Model and scaffold procedures, so students learn to work effectively in a variety of classroom configurations and activities. • Use various practices to differentiate instruction (e.g., cooperative learning, literature circles, partner work, and research/investigation groups).	• Use evidence-based rationale to make and monitor flexible instructional grouping options for students. • Model and scaffold procedures, so students learn to work effectively in a variety of classroom configurations and activities. • Use various practices to differentiate instruction (e.g., cooperative learning, partner work, and research/investigation groups).

Middle and High School Reading Classroom Teacher Candidates	Reading Specialist/Literacy Coach Candidates	Teacher Educator Candidates	Administrator Candidates
• Arrange their classrooms to provide easy access to books, other instructional materials, and specific areas designed for a variety of individual, small-group, and whole-class activities. • Modify the arrangements to accommodate students' changing needs.	• Arrange instructional areas to provide easy access to books and other instructional materials for a variety of individual, small-group, and whole-class activities and support teachers in doing the same. • Modify the arrangements to accommodate students' changing needs.	• Arrange the university classrooms in ways that facilitate understanding the role of the physical environment in reading and writing instruction.	• Provide resources and encourage flexibility in creating the physical environments.
• Demonstrate a respectful attitude toward all learners and understand the roles of choice, motivation, and scaffolded support in creating low-risk and positive social environments. • Model and teach students routines necessary for establishing and maintaining positive social environments (e.g., appropriate ways to interact with each other and adults). • Create supportive environments where English learners are encouraged and given many opportunities to use English.	• Create supportive social environments for all students, especially those who struggle with reading and writing. • Model for and support teachers and other professionals in doing the same for all students. • Create supportive environments where English learners are encouraged and provided with many opportunities to use English.	• Create positive social environments in the higher education classrooms. • Provide opportunities to create positive social environments. • Collaborate with candidates, colleagues, teachers, and other professionals to create positive social environments at the university and in schools, including supportive environments where English learners are given many opportunities to use English.	• Foster school climates that consistently demand positive social interactions between and among adults and students.
• Understand the role of routines in creating and maintaining positive learning environments for reading and writing instruction using traditional print, digital, and online resources. • Create and use routines to support instructional and social goals (e.g., regular steps for sharing and responding to materials read, formats for reporting, and efficient transitions among activities, spaces, and online resources).	• Understand the role of routines in creating and maintaining positive learning environments for reading and writing instruction using traditional print, digital, and online resources. • Create effective routines for all students, especially those who struggle with reading and writing. • Support teachers in doing the same for all readers.	• Create effective classroom routines in the higher education classrooms. • Provide opportunities for candidates and reading professionals to create and use classroom routines. • Collaborate with colleagues, teachers, and other professionals to incorporate the use of technology at the university and in schools.	• Understand how classroom routines can facilitate reading and writing instruction. • Provide school-level infrastructures that support the use of effective classroom routines.
• Use evidence-based rationale to make and monitor flexible instructional grouping options for students. • Model and scaffold procedures, so students learn to work effectively in a variety of classroom configurations and activities. • Use various practices to differentiate instruction (e.g., cooperative learning, literature circles, partner work, and research/investigation groups).	• Use evidence-based grouping practices to meet the needs of all students, especially those who struggle with reading and writing. • Support teachers in doing the same for all students.	• Prepare reading professionals to use evidence-based instructional grouping options for students. • Provide evidence-based information that supports different models of classroom organization and their relative benefits and limitations.	• Provide resources and encourage flexibility in differentiating instruction. • Recruit community members as mentors, tutors, volunteers, and resource providers to support literacy growth at the schools.

Standard 6: Professional Learning and Leadership

Element	Evidence that demonstrates competence may include, but is not limited to, the following:		
Candidates...	Education Support Personnel Candidates	Pre-K and Elementary Classroom Teacher Candidates	Middle and High School Content Classroom Teacher Candidates
6.1: Demonstrate foundational knowledge of adult learning theories and related research about organizational change, professional development, and school culture.	Not applicable	• Demonstrate an awareness of the factors that influence adult learning, organizational change, professional development, and school culture.	• Demonstrate awareness of the factors that influence adult learning, organizational change, professional development, and school culture.
6.2: Display positive dispositions related to their own reading and writing and the teaching of reading and writing, and pursue the development of individual professional knowledge and behaviors.	• Respect the importance of confidentiality. • Care for the well-being of students. • Demonstrate a belief that all students can learn. • Demonstrate a curiosity and interest in practice that results in student learning.	• Display positive reading and writing behaviors and serve as a model for students. • Promote student appreciation of the value of reading traditional print, digital, and online resources in and out of school. • Work collaboratively and respectfully with families, colleagues, and community members to support students' reading and writing. • Identify specific questions and goals about the teaching of reading and writing and plan specific strategies for finding answers to questions. • Implement plans and use results for their own professional growth. • Join professional organizations related to reading and writing and participate as members. • Demonstrate effective use of technology for improving student learning.	• Display positive reading and writing behaviors and serve as models for students. • Display positive dispositions related to their own reading and writing and use reading and writing to promote student learning. • Help students meet the specific demands of traditional print, digital, and online resources required for content learning. • Promote student understanding of the value of reading traditional print, digital, and online resources in and out of school. • Identify specific questions and goals about literacy and the learning of content and plan strategies for finding answers to questions. • Implement plans and use results for their own growth. • Are members of professional content area organizations. • Demonstrate effective use of technology for improving student learning.

Middle and High School Reading Classroom Teacher Candidates	Reading Specialist/Literacy Coach Candidates	Teacher Educator Candidates	Administrator Candidates
• Demonstrate an awareness of the factors that influence adult learning, organizational change, professional development, and school culture.	• Use literature and research findings about adult learning, organizational change, professional development, and school culture in working with teachers and other professionals. • Use knowledge of students and teachers to build effective professional development programs. • Use the research base to assist in building an effective, schoolwide professional development program.	• Examine and critique the literature on organizational change, adult learning, professional development, and school culture. • Have knowledge of interinstitutional collaboration and cooperation.	• Connect foundational knowledge associated with educational leadership to the organizational and instructional knowledge required to implement effective, schoolwide reading programs. • Apply knowledge from a variety of disciplines to promote positive school cultures and climates for students and adults.
• Display positive reading and writing behaviors and serve as models for students. • Understand the families' and community's roles in helping students apply reading and writing skills to content learning. • Work with families, colleagues, and the community to support student learning. • Promote student understanding of the value of reading traditional print, digital, and online resources in and out of school. • Identify specific questions and goals about the teaching of reading and writing and plan specific strategies for finding answers to those questions. • Carry out plans and use results for their own professional growth. • Are members of professional organizations related to reading and writing. • Demonstrate effective use of technology for improving student learning.	• Articulate the research base related to the connections among teacher dispositions, student learning, and the involvement of parents, guardians, and the community. • Promote the value of reading and writing in and out of school by modeling a positive attitude toward reading and writing with students, colleagues, administrators, and parents and guardians. • Join and participate in professional literacy organizations, symposia, conferences, and workshops. • Demonstrate effective interpersonal, communication, and leadership skills. • Demonstrate effective use of technology for improving student learning.	• Promote a positive and ethical learning environment with an emphasis on collaboration and respect that responds to students, families, teachers, and communities. • Demonstrate strong interpersonal and communication skills, as evident in interactions with all stakeholders. • Provide opportunities for candidates and reading professionals to share their own reading and writing. • Conduct research and communicate results for appropriate purposes and audiences. • Join and regularly participate in professional literacy organizations, conferences, symposia, and workshops. • Prepare and coach candidates and reading professionals to use various forms of research to inform practice.	• Ensure positive and ethical learning contexts for reading that respect students, families, teachers, colleagues, and communities. • Foster community involvement in schoolwide literacy initiatives. • Encourage and support teachers and reading professionals to develop their knowledge, skills, and dispositions. • Provide leadership by participating in ongoing professional development with staff and others in leadership positions. • Encourage use of technology among teachers and other personnel for their own learning and for improving student learning.

(continued)

Standard 6: Professional Learning and Leadership *(continued)*

Element	Evidence that demonstrates competence may include, but is not limited to, the following:			
Candidates...	Education Support Personnel Candidates	Pre-K and Elementary Classroom Teacher Candidates	Middle and High School Content Classroom Teacher Candidates	
6.3: Participate in, design, facilitate, lead, and evaluate effective and differentiated professional development programs.	• Participate with teachers in professional development experiences designed to improve student learning.	• Recognize the importance of professional development for improving reading and writing in schools. • Participate individually and with colleagues in professional development programs at the school and district levels. • Apply learning from professional development to instructional practices.	• Recognize the importance of professional development for improving academic learning through reading and writing in schools. • Participate individually and with colleagues in professional development programs at the school and district levels. • Apply learning from professional development to instructional practices.	
6.4: Understand and influence local, state, or national policy decisions.	• Recognize that policy mandates influence their responsibilities.	• Are informed about important professional issues. • Advocate with various groups (e.g., administrators, school boards, and local, state, and federal policymaking bodies) for needed organizational and instructional changes.	• Are informed about important professional issues. • Advocate with various groups (e.g., administrators, school boards, and local, state, and federal policymaking bodies) for needed organizational and instructional changes to promote effective literacy instruction.	

Middle and High School Reading Classroom Teacher Candidates	Reading Specialist/Literacy Coach Candidates	Teacher Educator Candidates	Administrator Candidates
• Recognize the importance of professional development for improving reading and writing in schools. • Participate individually and with colleagues in professional development programs at the school and district levels. • Apply learning from professional development to instructional practices.	• Collaborate in, leading, and evaluating professional development activities for individuals and groups of teachers. Activities may include working individually with teachers (e.g., modeling, coplanning, coteaching, and observing) or with groups (e.g., teacher workshops, group meetings, and online learning). • Demonstrate the ability to hold effective conversations (e.g., for planning and reflective problem solving) with individuals and groups of teachers, work collaboratively with teachers and administrators, and facilitate group meetings. • Support teachers in their efforts to use technology in literacy assessment and instruction.	• Know and critique the research on professional development. • Prepare and coach reading professionals to collaboratively plan, lead, and evaluate professional development activities at the grade, school, district, community, and state levels. • Participate in professional development at the national level through attendance and presentation at professional meetings, conferences, and symposia.	• Work collaboratively with school staff to plan, implement, and evaluate sustained professional development programs to meet established needs at grade, discipline, and individual levels. • Provide varied professional development opportunities for those having responsibility for student learning.
• Are informed about important professional issues. • Advocate with various groups (e.g., administrators, school boards, and local, state, and federal policymaking bodies) for needed organizational and instructional changes to promote effective literacy instruction.	• Demonstrate an understanding of local, state, and national policies that affect reading and writing instruction. • Write or assist in writing proposals that enable schools to obtain additional funding to support literacy efforts. • Promote effective communication and collaboration among stakeholders, including parents and guardians, teachers, administrators, policymakers, and community members. • Advocate with various groups (e.g., administrators, school boards, and local, state, and federal policymaking bodies) for needed organizational and instructional changes to promote effective literacy instruction.	• Read and critique the literature about state and federal initiatives that have implications for reading and writing instruction. • Provide opportunities for candidates and reading professionals to learn about these initiatives and their implications for reading and writing instruction. • Advocate with various groups (e.g., administrators, school boards, and local, state, and federal policymaking bodies) for needed organizational and instructional changes to promote effective literacy instruction.	• Promote effective communication and collaboration among parents and guardians, community members, and school staff. • Understand the importance of hiring highly qualified literacy personnel, providing clear role descriptions for literacy positions, and supporting individuals in those positions. • Advocate at local, state, and federal levels for needed organizational and instructional changes to promote effective literacy instruction.

Role Descriptions, Elements, and Evidence That Demonstrates Competence

Education Support Personnel

Education Support Personnel assist classroom teachers and Reading Specialist/ Literacy Coaches in delivering reading instruction and collaborate with reading professionals to improve reading achievement in the schools in which they work. Education Support Personnel assist in general education, special education, or reading and writing education in graded or age-grouped classrooms at the pre-K–12 levels and in before-school, after-school, or summer school reading programs. They may also have responsibilities for preparing instructional materials, keeping records, or assisting with student assessments.

For certification, an Education Support Personnel Candidate must have the following:

- Two years of preparation at an institution of higher education or completion of an associates' degree

- Attended a program that includes reading and reading-related courses (e.g., language and literacy development, and child development)

Standard 1: Foundational Knowledge	Candidates understand the theoretical and evidence-based foundations of reading and writing processes and instruction
Elements	Evidence that demonstrates competence may include, but is not limited to, the following—Education Support Personnel Candidates...
1.1: Understand major theories and empirical research that describe the cognitive, linguistic, motivational, and sociocultural foundations of reading and writing development, processes, and components, including word recognition, language comprehension, strategic knowledge, and reading–writing connections.	• Identify examples of reading instruction for developing word recognition, language comprehension, strategic knowledge, and reading–writing connections.[a] • Identify conditions that support individual motivation to read and write (e.g., access to print, choice, challenge, interests, and family and community knowledge) as factors that enhance literacy learning for all.
1.2: Understand the historically shared knowledge of the profession and changes over time in the perceptions of reading and writing development, processes, and components.	Not applicable
1.3: Understand the role of professional judgment and practical knowledge for improving all students' reading development and achievement.	• Show fair-mindedness, empathy, and ethical behavior when teaching students and working with other professionals.

[a]McKenna and Stahl (2009) define *reading* as including word recognition, language comprehension, and strategic knowledge (see the Glossary for their definition of *cognitive model of reading*).

Standard 2: Curriculum and Instruction	Candidates use instructional approaches, materials, and an integrated, comprehensive, balanced curriculum to support student learning in reading and writing.
Elements	Evidence that demonstrates competence may include, but is not limited to, the following—Education Support Personnel Candidates…
2.1: Use foundational knowledge to design or implement an integrated, comprehensive, and balanced curriculum.	• Implement lessons that are part of the reading and writing curriculum with teacher guidance and supervision.
2.2: Use appropriate and varied instructional approaches, including those that develop word recognition, language comprehension, strategic knowledge, and reading–writing connections.	• Use a wide range of instructional approaches selected and supervised by the teacher.
2.3: Use a wide range of texts (e.g., narrative, expository, and poetry) from traditional print, digital, and online resources.	• With guidance from teachers, select and use a wide range of materials.

Standard 3: Assessment and Evaluation	Candidates use a variety of assessment tools and practices to plan and evaluate effective reading and writing instruction.
Elements	Evidence that demonstrates competence may include, but is not limited to, the following—Education Support Personnel Candidates…
3.1: Understand types of assessments and their purposes, strengths, and limitations.	• Demonstrate an understanding of established purposes for assessing student performance.
3.2: Select, develop, administer, and interpret assessments, both traditional print and electronic, for specific purposes.	• Administer assessments under the direction of certified personnel.
3.3: Use assessment information to plan and evaluate instruction.	• Support teachers in data collection and record keeping.
3.4: Communicate assessment results and implications to a variety of audiences.	• Understand the importance of student confidentiality and acknowledge the role of certified personnel as communicators of assessment results.

Standard 4: Diversity	Candidates create and engage their students in literacy practices that develop awareness, understanding, respect, and a valuing of differences in our society.
Elements	Evidence that demonstrates competence may include, but is not limited to, the following—Education Support Personnel Candidates…
4.1: Recognize, understand, and value the forms of diversity that exist in society and their importance in learning to read and write.	• Recognize the forms of diversity in their own lives and understand how these may limit or enable their reading and writing. • Demonstrate an understanding of the forms of diversity that exist in society, with a particular focus on individual and group differences that have been used to marginalize some and privilege others. • Value diversity as a resource in a functioning democratic society.
4.2: Use a literacy curriculum and engage in instructional practices that positively impact students' knowledge, beliefs, and engagement with the features of diversity.	• Describe specific aspects of school and community experiences that can be used to reveal students' diversity and engage them in learning. • Assist in instructional practices that are linked to students' diversity and which also acquaint them with others' traditions and diversity. • Assist in instructional practices that engage students as agents of their own learning.
4.3: Develop and implement strategies to advocate for equity.	• Use their literacy skills to assist communities that are experiencing discrimination to overcome it (e.g., volunteer in the development of or teach in an adult literacy or English as a second language program).

Standard 5: Literate Environment	Candidates create a literate environment that fosters reading and writing by integrating foundational knowledge, instructional practices, approaches and methods, curriculum materials, and the appropriate use of assessments.
Elements	**Evidence that demonstrates competence may include, but is not limited to, the following—Education Support Personnel Candidates…**
5.1: Design the physical environment to optimize students' use of traditional print, digital, and online resources in reading and writing instruction.	• Assist classroom teachers in developing and maintaining physical arrangements of traditional print, digital, and online resources that facilitate reading and writing instruction.
5.2: Design a social environment that is low risk and includes choice, motivation, and scaffolded support to optimize students' opportunities for learning to read and write.	• Assist classroom teachers in creating and maintaining positive social environments.
5.3: Use routines to support reading and writing instruction (e.g., time allocation, transitions from one activity to another; discussions, and peer feedback).	• Understand how and why classroom teachers use specific routines. • Assist classroom teachers in creating and maintaining those routines.
5.4: Use a variety of classroom configurations (i.e., whole class, small group, and individual) to differentiate instruction.	• Use a variety of instructional grouping options selected by and supervised by the classroom teachers. • In consultation with the teachers, adjust instructional groupings to ensure that the diverse needs of learners are being met.

Standard 6: Professional Learning and Leadership	Candidates recognize the importance of, demonstrate, and facilitate professional learning and leadership as a career-long effort and responsibility.
Elements	**Evidence that demonstrates competence may include, but is not limited to, the following—Education Support Personnel Candidates…**
6.1: Demonstrate foundational knowledge of adult learning theories and related research about organizational change, professional development, and school culture.	Not applicable
6.2: Display positive dispositions related to their own reading and writing and the teaching of reading and writing, and pursue the development of individual professional knowledge and behaviors.	• Respect the importance of confidentiality. • Care for the well-being of students. • Demonstrate a belief that all students can learn. • Demonstrate a curiosity and interest in practice that results in student learning.
6.3: Participate in, design, facilitate, lead, and evaluate effective and differentiated professional development programs.	• Participate with teachers in professional development experiences designed to improve student learning.
6.4: Understand and influence local, state, or national policy decisions.	• Recognize that policy mandates influence their responsibilities.

Pre-K and Elementary Classroom Teacher

Pre-K and Elementary Classroom Teachers are professionals responsible for teaching reading and writing to students in either a self-contained or departmentalized setting at the pre-K or elementary levels. These professionals may also be responsible for teaching content such as social studies or science. Regardless of their role, these individuals must be able to provide effective instruction for all students in the classroom, from those who struggle with learning to read to those who need enrichment experiences. These teachers collaborate with reading specialists and other professionals to improve instruction and to modify the physical and social environments as needed.

For certification, a Pre-K and Elementary Classroom Teacher Candidate must have the following:

- An undergraduate or graduate degree with a major in early childhood/ elementary education

- Reading and reading-related course work (typically 9–12 credits) that enables the candidate to demonstrate mastery of elements identified in *Standards 2010*

Standard 1: Foundational Knowledge	Candidates understand the theoretical and evidence-based foundations of reading and writing processes and instruction.
Elements	Evidence that demonstrates competence may include, but is not limited to, the following—Pre-K and Elementary Classroom Teacher Candidates…
1.1: Understand major theories and empirical research that describe the cognitive, linguistic, motivational, and sociocultural foundations of reading and writing development, processes, and components, including word recognition, language comprehension, strategic knowledge, and reading–writing connections.	• Recognize major theories of reading and writing processes and development, including first and second literacy acquisition and the role of native language in learning to read and write in a second language. • Explain language and reading development across elementary years (e.g., word recognition, language comprehension, strategic knowledge, and reading–writing connections) using supporting evidence from theory and research.[a] • Demonstrate knowledge about transfer of skills from the primary or home language (L1) to English (L2) as it affects literacy learning across these components. • Explain the research and theory about effective learning environments that support individual motivation to read and write (e.g., choice, challenge, interests, and access to traditional print, digital, and online resources).
1.2: Understand the historically shared knowledge of the profession and changes over time in the perceptions of reading and writing development, processes, and components.	• Identify major milestones in reading scholarship and interpret them in light of the current social context.
1.3: Understand the role of professional judgment and practical knowledge for improving all students' reading development and achievement.	• Show fair-mindedness, empathy, and ethical behavior in literacy instruction and when working with other professionals. • Use multiple sources of information to guide instructional planning to improve reading achievement of all students.

[a]McKenna and Stahl (2009) define *reading* as including word recognition, language comprehension, and strategic knowledge (see the Glossary for their definition of *cognitive model of reading*).

Standard 2: Curriculum and Instruction	Candidates use instructional approaches, materials, and an integrated, comprehensive, balanced curriculum to support student learning in reading and writing.
Elements	**Evidence that demonstrates competence may include, but is not limited to, the following—Pre-K and Elementary Classroom Teacher Candidates...**
2.1: Use foundational knowledge to design or implement an integrated, comprehensive, and balanced curriculum.	• Explain how the reading and writing curriculum is related to local, state, and professional standards. • Implement the curriculum based on students' prior knowledge, world experiences, and interests. • Evaluate the curriculum to ensure that instructional goals and objectives are met. • Plan with other teachers and support personnel in designing, adjusting, and modifying the curriculum to meet students' needs in traditional print, digital, and online contexts.
2.2: Use appropriate and varied instructional approaches, including those that develop word recognition, language comprehension, strategic knowledge, and reading–writing connections.	• Select and implement instructional approaches based on evidence-based rationale, student needs, and purposes for instruction. • Differentiate instructional approaches to meet students' reading and writing needs. • Implement and evaluate instruction in each of the following areas: concepts of print, phonemic awareness, phonics, vocabulary, comprehension, fluency, critical thinking, motivation, and writing. • Incorporate traditional print, digital, and online resources as instructional tools to enhance student learning. • As needed, adapt instructional approaches and materials to meet the language-proficiency needs of English learners.
2.3: Use a wide range of texts (e.g., narrative, expository, and poetry) from traditional print, digital, and online resources.	• Guided by evidence-based rationale, select and use quality traditional print, digital, and online resources. • Build an accessible, multilevel, and diverse classroom library that contains traditional print, digital, and online classroom materials.

Standard 3: Assessment and Evaluation	Candidates use a variety of assessment tools and practices to plan and evaluate effective reading and writing instruction.
Elements	**Evidence that demonstrates competence may include, but is not limited to, the following—Pre-K and Elementary Classroom Teacher Candidates...**
3.1: Understand types of assessments and their purposes, strengths, and limitations.	• Demonstrate an understanding of established purposes for assessing student performance, including tools for screening, diagnosis, progress monitoring, and measuring outcomes. • Describe strengths and limitations of a range of assessment tools and their appropriate uses. • Recognize the basic technical adequacy of assessments (e.g., reliability, content, and construct validity). • Explain district and state assessment frameworks, proficiency standards, and student benchmarks.
3.2: Select, develop, administer, and interpret assessments, both traditional print and electronic, for specific purposes.	• Select or develop appropriate assessment tools to monitor student progress and to analyze instructional effectiveness.[a] • Administer classroom and school-based assessments using consistent, fair, and equitable assessment procedures. • Interpret and use assessment data to analyze individual, group, and classroom performance and progress. • Collaborate with other teachers and with support personnel to discuss interpretation of assessment data and their uses in responding to student needs and strengths.
3.3: Use assessment information to plan and evaluate instruction.	• Use assessment data to plan instruction systematically and to select appropriate traditional print, digital, and online reading resources. • Use assessment data to evaluate students' responses to instruction and to develop relevant next steps for teaching. • Interpret patterns in classroom and individual students' data. • Collaborate with other reading professionals to modify instruction and to plan and evaluate interventions based on assessment data.
3.4: Communicate assessment results and implications to a variety of audiences.	• Communicate assessment purposes and a summary of results to appropriate audiences (i.e., student, parents or guardians, colleagues, and administrators). • Use assessment data and student work samples to discuss relevant implications and goals for reading and writing instruction.

[a]These tools may include standardized or more subjective measures, such as rubrics, observations, surveys, and anecdotal records.

Standard 4: Diversity	Candidates create and engage their students in literacy practices that develop awareness, understanding, respect, and a valuing of differences in our society.
Elements	**Evidence that demonstrates competence may include, but is not limited to, the following—Pre-K and Elementary Classroom Teacher Candidates…**
4.1: Recognize, understand, and value the forms of diversity that exist in society and their importance in learning to read and write.	• Demonstrate an understanding of the ways in which diversity can be used to strengthen a literate society, making it more productive, more adaptable to change, and more equitable. • Demonstrate an understanding of the impact of urban, suburban, and rural environments on local culture, language, and learning to read and write. • Demonstrate an understanding of the ways in which the various forms of diversity interact with reading and writing development. • Demonstrate an understanding of the relationship between first- and second-language acquisition and literacy development.
4.2: Use a literacy curriculum and engage in instructional practices that positively impact students' knowledge, beliefs, and engagement with the features of diversity.	• Assess the various forms of diversity that exist in students as well as in the surrounding community. • Provide differentiated instruction and instructional materials, including traditional print, digital, and online resources, that capitalize on diversity. • Provide instruction and instructional materials that are linked to students' backgrounds and facilitate a learning environment in which differences and commonalities are valued (e.g., use literature that reflects the experiences of marginalized groups and the strategies they use to overcome challenges). • Provide instruction and instructional formats that engage students as agents of their own learning.
4.3: Develop and implement strategies to advocate for equity.	• Provide students with linguistic, academic, and cultural experiences that link their communities with the school. • Advocate for change in societal practices and institutional structures that are inherently biased or prejudiced against certain groups. • Demonstrate how issues of inequity and opportunities for social justice activism and resiliency can be incorporated into the literacy curriculum.

Standard 5: Literate Environment	Candidates create a literate environment that fosters reading and writing by integrating foundational knowledge, instructional practices, approaches and methods, curriculum materials, and the appropriate use of assessments.
Elements	**Evidence that demonstrates competence may include, but is not limited to, the following—Pre-K and Elementary Classroom Teacher Candidates…**
5.1: Design the physical environment to optimize students' use of traditional print, digital, and online resources in reading and writing instruction.	• Arrange their classrooms to provide easy access to books, other materials, and specific areas designed for a variety of individual, small-group, and whole-class activities. • Modify the arrangements to accommodate students' changing needs.
5.2: Design a social environment that is low risk and includes choice, motivation, and scaffolded support to optimize students' opportunities for learning to read and write.	• Demonstrate a respectful attitude toward all learners and understand the roles of choice, motivation, and scaffolded support in creating low-risk and positive social environments. • Model and teach students routines for establishing and maintaining positive social environments (e.g., appropriate ways to interact with each other and adults). • Create supportive environments where English learners are encouraged and given many opportunities to use English.
5.3: Use routines to support reading and writing instruction (e.g., time allocation, transitions from one activity to another; discussions, and peer feedback).	• Understand the role of routines in creating and maintaining positive learning environments for reading and writing instruction using traditional print, digital, and online resources. • Create and use routines to support instructional and social goals (e.g., regular steps for sharing and responding to stories, formats for reporting, and efficient transitions among activities, spaces, and online resources).
5.4: Use a variety of classroom configurations (i.e., whole class, small group, and individual) to differentiate instruction.	• Use evidence-based rationale to make and monitor flexible instructional grouping options for students. • Model and scaffold procedures, so students learn to work effectively in a variety of classroom configurations and activities. • Use various practices to differentiate instruction (e.g., cooperative learning, literature circles, partner work, and research/investigation groups).

Standard 6: Professional Learning and Leadership	Candidates recognize the importance of, demonstrate, and facilitate professional learning and leadership as a career-long effort and responsibility.
Elements	**Evidence that demonstrates competence may include, but is not limited to, the following—Pre-K and Elementary Classroom Teacher Candidates...**
6.1: Demonstrate foundational knowledge of adult learning theories and related research about organizational change, professional development, and school culture.	• Demonstrate an awareness of the factors that influence adult learning, organizational change, professional development, and school culture.
6.2: Display positive dispositions related to their own reading and writing and the teaching of reading and writing, and pursue the development of individual professional knowledge and behaviors.	• Display positive reading and writing behaviors and serve as a model for students. • Promote student appreciation of the value of reading traditional print, digital, and online resources in and out of school. • Work collaboratively and respectfully with families, colleagues, and community members to support students' reading and writing. • Identify specific questions and goals about the teaching of reading and writing and plan specific strategies for finding answers to questions. • Implement plans and use results for their own professional growth. • Join professional organizations related to reading and writing and participate as members. • Demonstrate effective use of technology for improving student learning.
6.3: Participate in, design, facilitate, lead, and evaluate effective and differentiated professional development programs.	• Recognize the importance of professional development for improving reading and writing in schools. • Participate individually and with colleagues in professional development programs at the school and district levels. • Apply learning from professional development to instructional practices.
6.4: Understand and influence local, state, or national policy decisions.	• Are informed about important professional issues. • Advocate with various groups (e.g., administrators, school boards, and local, state, and federal policymaking bodies) for needed organizational and instructional changes.

Middle and High School Content Classroom Teacher

A Middle and High School Content Classroom Teacher is a professional responsible for teaching one of the content or academic areas (e.g., science, mathematics, social studies, or English) at either the middle or high school level. These teachers must teach the content of the discipline and have responsibility for helping students engage in and learn not only the content but also the reading and writing demands of the discipline. Middle and High School Content Classroom Teachers collaborate with reading specialists and other professionals to improve instruction and to modify the physical and social environments as needed.

For certification, a Middle and High School Classroom Teacher Candidate must have the following:

• An undergraduate or graduate degree with a major in the specific academic discipline

• Successful completion of content area reading or adolescent literacy courses as part of the degree

Standard 1: Foundational Knowledge	Candidates understand the theoretical and evidence-based foundations of reading and writing processes and instruction.
Elements	Evidence that demonstrates competence may include, but is not limited to, the following—Middle and High School Content Classroom Teacher Candidates…
1.1: Understand major theories and empirical research that describe the cognitive, linguistic, motivational, and sociocultural foundations of reading and writing development, processes, and components, including word recognition, language comprehension, strategic knowledge, and reading–writing connections.	• Recognize major theories and research evidence of reading and writing processes and development in adolescence, including first and second literacy acquisition and the role of native language in learning to read and write in a second language. • Identify and explain the specific reading and writing expectations of their content areas as described in national and state standards. • Explain the research and theory of learning environments that support individual motivation to read and write.[a] • Value the scholarship of the reading profession and seek to understand the theoretical knowledge base in relation to their disciplinary areas. • Understand the process of identifying and differentiating the range of literacy needs of adolescent readers.
1.2: Understand the historically shared knowledge of the profession and changes over time in the perceptions of reading and writing development, processes, and components.	Not applicable
1.3: Understand the role of professional judgment and practical knowledge for improving all students' reading development and achievement.	• Show fair-mindedness, empathy, and ethical behavior when teaching students and working with other professionals. • Use multiple sources of information to guide instructional planning to improve reading achievement of all students.

[a]For example, choice, challenge, interests, and access to traditional print, digital, and online resources.

Standard 2: Curriculum and Instruction	Candidates use instructional approaches, materials, and an integrated, comprehensive, balanced curriculum to support student learning in reading and writing.
Elements	Evidence that demonstrates competence may include, but is not limited to, the following—Middle and High School Content Classroom Teacher Candidates…
2.1: Use foundational knowledge to design or implement an integrated, comprehensive, and balanced curriculum.	• Explain how reading and writing relate to their content areas and to local, state, and professional standards. • Implement the curriculum based on students' prior knowledge, world experiences, and interests. • Evaluate the curriculum to ensure that instructional goals and objectives meet the reading and writing demands of the content areas. • Work with other teachers and support personnel to design, adjust, and modify the curriculum to meet students' literacy needs. • Support students as agents of their own learning and critical consumers of the discipline.
2.2: Use appropriate and varied instructional approaches, including those that develop word recognition, language comprehension, strategic knowledge, and reading–writing connections.	• Select and implement content area reading and writing instructional approaches based on evidence-based rationale, student needs, and purposes for instruction. • Differentiate instructional approaches to meet students' reading and writing needs in the content areas.[a] • Implement and evaluate content area instruction in each of the following areas: vocabulary meaning, comprehension, writing, motivation, and critical thinking.[b] • Incorporate traditional print, digital, and online resources as instructional tools to enhance student learning. • As needed, adapt instructional approaches and materials to meet the language-proficiency needs of English learners.
2.3: Use a wide range of texts (e.g., narrative, expository, and poetry) from traditional print, digital, and online resources.	• Demonstrate knowledge about various materials and their uses. • Guided by evidence-based rationale, select and use quality traditional print, digital, and online resources. • Build an accessible, multilevel, and diverse classroom library for their content areas that contains traditional print, digital, and online resources.

[a]Literacy development is an ongoing process and requires as much attention for adolescents as for beginning readers. Literacy demands are expanding and include more reading and writing tasks than in the past (see IRA's position statement on adolescent literacy for more information at www.reading.org/General/AboutIRA/PositionStatements/AdolescentLitPosition.aspx). [b]Vocabulary meaning instruction should include work with multisyllabic words and the use of affixes and Greek and Latin roots.

Standard 3: Assessment and Evaluation	Candidates use a variety of assessment tools and practices to plan and evaluate effective reading and writing instruction.
Elements	**Evidence that demonstrates competence may include, but is not limited to, the following—Middle and High School Content Classroom Teacher Candidates…**
3.1: Understand types of assessments and their purposes, strengths, and limitations.	• Demonstrate an understanding of reading and writing elements of content area assessments and their purposes in assessing student performance. • Describe the strengths and limitations of a range of assessment tools and their appropriate uses. • Recognize the basic technical adequacy of assessments (e.g., reliability, content, and construct validity). • Explain district and state assessment frameworks, proficiency standards, and student benchmarks.
3.2: Select, develop, administer, and interpret assessments, both traditional print and electronic, for specific purposes.	• Select or develop assessment tools to analyze instructional effectiveness within the content areas. • Administer classroom and school-based assessments using consistent, fair, and equitable assessment procedures. • Interpret and use assessment data to analyze individual, group, and classroom performance and progress. • Collaborate with other teachers and with support personnel to discuss interpretation of assessment data and their uses in responding to student needs and strengths.
3.3: Use assessment information to plan and evaluate instruction.	• Analyze and use assessment data to plan and adjust instruction systematically and to select appropriate reading materials for use in the content areas. • Analyze and use assessment data to evaluate students' responses to instruction and to develop relevant next steps for teaching. • Identify and interpret patterns in classroom and individual students' data. • Collaborate with reading teachers to identify relevant reading and writing strategies and skills for use in the specific content areas or disciplines.
3.4: Communicate assessment results and implications to a variety of audiences.	• Communicate assessment purposes and a summary of results to appropriate audiences (i.e., student, parents or guardians, colleagues, and administrators). • Use assessment data and student work samples to discuss implications for the content areas or literacy instruction (e.g., highlight differences in student work samples across a content area).

Standard 4: Diversity	Candidates create and engage their students in literacy practices that develop awareness, understanding, respect, and a valuing of differences in our society.
Elements	**Evidence that demonstrates competence may include, but is not limited to, the following—Middle and High School Content Classroom Teacher Candidates…**
4.1: Recognize, understand, and value the forms of diversity that exist in society and their importance in learning to read and write.	• Demonstrate an understanding of the ways in which diversity can be used to strengthen a literate society, making it more productive, more adaptable to change, and more equitable. • Demonstrate an understanding of the impact of urban, suburban, and rural environments on local culture, language, and learning to read and write. • Demonstrate an understanding of the ways in which various forms of diversity interact with adolescent literacy development and content area learning. • Demonstrate an understanding of the relationship between first- and second-language acquisition and literacy development.
4.2: Use a literacy curriculum and engage in instructional practices that positively impact students' knowledge, beliefs, and engagement with the features of diversity.	• Assess the various forms of diversity that exist in students as well as in the surrounding community. • Provide differentiated instruction and instructional materials, including traditional print, digital, and online resources, that capitalize on diversity. • Provide instructional formats that engage students as agents of their own learning.
4.3: Develop and implement strategies to advocate for equity.	• Provide students with linguistic, academic, and cultural experiences that link their backgrounds with content area learning. • Advocate for change in societal practices and institutional structures that are inherently biased or prejudiced against certain groups. • Demonstrate how issues of inequity and opportunities for social justice activism and resiliency in students' communities can be incorporated into the content areas and literacy curriculum.

Standard 5: Literate Environment	Candidates create a literate environment that fosters reading and writing by integrating foundational knowledge, instructional practices, approaches and methods, curriculum materials, and the appropriate use of assessments.
Elements	**Evidence that demonstrates competence may include, but is not limited to, the following—Middle and High School Content Classroom Teacher Candidates…**
5.1: Design the physical environment to optimize students' use of traditional print, digital, and online resources in reading and writing instruction.	• Arrange their classrooms to provide easy access to books, other instructional materials, and specific areas designed for a variety of individual, small-group, and whole-class activities. • Modify the arrangements to accommodate students' changing needs.
5.2: Design a social environment that is low risk and includes choice, motivation, and scaffolded support to optimize students' opportunities for learning to read and write.	• Demonstrate a respectful attitude toward all learners and understand the roles of choice, motivation, and scaffolded support in creating low-risk and positive social environments. • Model and teach students appropriate ways to interact with each other and adults. • Create supportive environments where English learners are encouraged and given many opportunities to use English.
5.3: Use routines to support reading and writing instruction (e.g., time allocation, transitions from one activity to another; discussions, and peer feedback).	• Understand the role of routines in creating and maintaining positive learning environments for content area learning using traditional print, digital, and online resources. • Create and use routines to support instructional and social goals (e.g., regular steps for sharing and responding to stories, formats for reporting, and efficient transitions among activities, spaces, and online resources).
5.4: Use a variety of classroom configurations (i.e., whole class, small group, and individual) to differentiate instruction.	• Use evidence-based rationale to make and monitor flexible instructional grouping options for students. • Model and scaffold procedures, so students learn to work effectively in a variety of classroom configurations and activities. • Use various practices to differentiate instruction (e.g., cooperative learning, partner work, and research/investigation groups).

Standard 6: Professional Learning and Leadership	Candidates recognize the importance of, demonstrate, and facilitate professional learning and leadership as a career-long effort and responsibility.
Elements	**Evidence that demonstrates competence may include, but is not limited to, the following—Middle and High School Content Classroom Teacher Candidates…**
6.1: Demonstrate foundational knowledge of adult learning theories and related research about organizational change, professional development, and school culture.	• Demonstrate awareness of the factors that influence adult learning, organizational change, professional development, and school culture.
6.2: Display positive dispositions related to their own reading and writing and the teaching of reading and writing, and pursue the development of individual professional knowledge and behaviors.	• Display positive reading and writing behaviors and serve as models for students. • Display positive dispositions related to their own reading and writing and use reading and writing to promote student learning. • Help students meet the specific demands of traditional print, digital, and online resources required for content learning. • Promote student understanding of the value of reading traditional print, digital, and online resources in and out of school. • Identify specific questions and goals about literacy and the learning of content and plan strategies for finding answers to questions. • Implement plans and use results for their own growth. • Are members of professional content area organizations. • Demonstrate effective use of technology for improving student learning.
6.3: Participate in, design, facilitate, lead, and evaluate effective and differentiated professional development programs.	• Recognize the importance of professional development for improving academic learning through reading and writing in schools. • Participate individually and with colleagues in professional development programs at the school and district levels. • Apply learning from professional development to instructional practices.
6.4: Understand and influence local, state, or national policy decisions.	• Are informed about important professional issues. • Advocate with various groups (e.g., administrators, school boards, and local, state, and federal policymaking bodies) for needed organizational and instructional changes to promote effective literacy instruction.

Middle and High School Reading Classroom Teacher

A Middle and High School Reading Classroom Teacher is a professional responsible for teaching reading at the middle or high school level for all or part of the day. Reading classroom teachers are responsible for teaching one or more reading classes and might have multiple responsibilities, such as teaching reading to students who would benefit from such instruction (e.g., increasing vocabulary and learning general study skills). Another responsibility would be to assess students to determine their reading needs and strengths. These professionals collaborate with reading specialists and other professionals to improve instruction and to modify the physical and social environments as needed.

For certification, a Middle and High School Reading Classroom Teacher Candidate must have the following:

- An undergraduate or graduate degree that includes a major in a specific discipline

- Additional reading and reading-related courses, typically 12–15 undergraduate or graduate credits, including adolescent literacy and teaching reading and writing in the content areas.

Standard 1: Foundational Knowledge	Candidates understand the theoretical and evidence-based foundations of reading and writing processes and instruction.
Elements	Evidence that demonstrates competence may include, but is not limited to, the following—Middle and High School Reading Classroom Teacher Candidates…
1.1: Understand major theories and empirical research that describe the cognitive, linguistic, motivational, and sociocultural foundations of reading and writing development, processes, and components, including word recognition, language comprehension, strategic knowledge, and reading–writing connections.	• Read the scholarship of the reading profession and recognize the theoretical knowledge base about the reading and writing of adolescents. • Explain major theories of reading and writing processes and development in adolescents using supporting research evidence, including the relationship between culture and the native language of English learners as a support system in their learning to read and write in English. • Explain language and reading development during adolescence (e.g., word recognition, language comprehension, strategic knowledge, and reading–writing connections) with supporting evidence from theory and research. • Explain the research and theory of learning environments that support individual motivation to read and write.[a]
1.2: Understand the historically shared knowledge of the profession and changes over time in the perceptions of reading and writing development, processes, and components.	• Identify major milestones in reading scholarship and interpret them in light of the current social context.
1.3: Understand the role of professional judgment and practical knowledge for improving all students' reading development and achievement.	• Show fair-mindedness, empathy, and ethical behavior when teaching students and working with other professionals. • Use multiple sources of information to guide instructional planning to improve reading achievement of all students.

[a]For example, access to traditional text, digital texts, media collaboration, choice, challenge, and interests.

Standard 2: Curriculum and Instruction	Candidates use instructional approaches, materials, and an integrated, comprehensive, balanced curriculum to support student learning in reading and writing.
Elements	**Evidence that demonstrates competence may include, but is not limited to, the following—Middle and High School Reading Classroom Teacher Candidates...**
2.1: Use foundational knowledge to design or implement an integrated, comprehensive, and balanced curriculum.	• Explain how reading and writing relates to their content area and the local, state, national, and professional standards. • Implement the curriculum based on students' prior knowledge, world experiences, and interests. • Evaluate the curriculum to ensure that instructional goals and objectives are met. • Work with the team or department to help ensure interdisciplinary connections in traditional print, digital, and online contexts.
2.2: Use appropriate and varied instructional approaches, including those that develop word recognition, language comprehension, strategic knowledge, and reading–writing connections.	• Select and implement reading and writing approaches that are evidence based and meet student needs. • Differentiate instructional approaches to meet students' reading and writing needs in the content areas.[a] • Implement and evaluate content area instruction in each of the following elements: vocabulary meaning, comprehension, writing, motivation, and critical thinking.[b] • Incorporate traditional print, digital, and online resources as instructional tools to enhance student learning. • As needed, adapt instructional approaches and materials to meet the language-proficiency needs of English learners.
2.3: Use a wide range of texts (e.g., narrative, expository, and poetry) from traditional print, digital, and online resources.	• Demonstrate knowledge about various materials, including those specifically for adolescent learners, and their uses. • Guided by evidence-based rationale, select and use traditional print, digital, and online resources. • Build an accessible, multilevel, and diverse classroom library that contains traditional print, digital, and online resources.

[a]Literacy development is an ongoing process and requires as much attention for adolescents as for beginning readers. Literacy demands are expanding and include more reading and writing tasks than in the past (see IRA's position statement on adolescent literacy for more information at www.reading.org/General/AboutIRA/PositionStatements/AdolescentLitPosition.aspx). [b]Vocabulary meaning instruction should include work with multisyllabic words and the use of affixes and Greek and Latin roots.

Standard 3: Assessment and Evaluation	Candidates use a variety of assessment tools and practices to plan and evaluate effective reading and writing instruction.
Elements	Evidence that demonstrates competence may include, but is not limited to, the following—Middle and High School Reading Classroom Teacher Candidates…
3.1: Understand types of assessments and their purposes, strengths, and limitations.	• Demonstrate an understanding of established purposes for assessing student performance, including tools for screening, diagnosis, progress monitoring, and measuring outcomes. • Describe the strengths and limitations of a range of assessment tools and their appropriate uses. • Recognize the basic technical adequacy of assessments (e.g., reliability, content, and construct validity). • Explain district and state assessment frameworks, proficiency standards, and student benchmarks.
3.2: Select, develop, administer, and interpret assessments, both traditional print and electronic, for specific purposes.	• Select or develop appropriate assessment tools to monitor student progress and to analyze instructional effectiveness.[a] • Administer classroom and school-based assessments using consistent, fair, and equitable assessment procedures. • Recommend and administer assessments for students in need of reading and writing assistance. • Interpret and use assessment data to analyze individual, group, and classroom performance and progress within and across content areas and disciplines. • Collaborate with content teachers to monitor student progress and to analyze instructional effectiveness.
3.3: Use assessment information to plan and evaluate instruction.	• Use assessment data to plan instruction systematically and to select appropriate traditional print, digital, and online reading resources. • Use assessment data to evaluate students' responses to instruction and to develop relevant next steps for teaching. • Identify and interpret patterns in classroom and individual students' data. • Collaborate with content area teachers to use assessment data to modify instruction, evaluate the effectiveness of instruction, and plan content literacy initiatives.
3.4: Communicate assessment results and implications to a variety of audiences.	• Communicate assessment purposes and discuss results with appropriate audiences (i.e., student, parents or guardians, colleagues, and administrators). • Use assessment data and student work samples to discuss implications for reading and writing instruction (e.g., highlight differences in student work samples across the content areas).

[a]These tools may include standardized or more subjective measures, such as rubrics, observations, surveys, and anecdotal records.

Standard 4: Diversity	Candidates create and engage their students in literacy practices that develop awareness, understanding, respect, and a valuing of differences in our society.
Elements	Evidence that demonstrates competence may include, but is not limited to, the following—Middle and High School Reading Classroom Teacher Candidates…
4.1: Recognize, understand, and value the forms of diversity that exist in society and their importance in learning to read and write.	• Demonstrate an understanding of the ways in which diversity can be used to strengthen a literate society, making it more productive, more adaptable to change, and more equitable. • Demonstrate an understanding of the impact of urban, suburban, and rural environments on local culture, language, and learning to read and write. • Demonstrate an understanding of the ways in which diversity influences adolescent literacy development. • Demonstrate an understanding of the relationship between first- and second-language acquisition and literacy development.
4.2: Use a literacy curriculum and engage in instructional practices that positively impact students' knowledge, beliefs, and engagement with the features of diversity.	• Assess the various forms of diversity that exist in students as well as in the surrounding community. • Provide differentiated instruction and instructional materials, including traditional print, digital, and online resources, that capitalize on diversity. • Provide instructional formats that engage students as agents of their own learning.
4.3: Develop and implement strategies to advocate for equity.	• Provide students with linguistic, academic, and cultural experiences that link their communities with the school. • Advocate for change in societal practices and institutional structures that are inherently biased or prejudiced against certain groups. • Demonstrate how issues of inequity and opportunities for social justice activism and resiliency can be incorporated into the literacy curriculum.

Standard 5: Literate Environment	Candidates create a literate environment that fosters reading and writing by integrating foundational knowledge, instructional practices, approaches and methods, curriculum materials, and the appropriate use of assessments.
Elements	Evidence that demonstrates competence may include, but is not limited to, the following—Middle and High School Reading Classroom Teacher Candidates…
5.1: Design the physical environment to optimize students' use of traditional print, digital, and online resources in reading and writing instruction.	• Arrange their classrooms to provide easy access to books, other instructional materials, and specific areas designed for a variety of individual, small-group, and whole-class activities. • Modify the arrangements to accommodate students' changing needs.
5.2: Design a social environment that is low risk and includes choice, motivation, and scaffolded support to optimize students' opportunities for learning to read and write.	• Demonstrate a respectful attitude toward all learners and understand the roles of choice, motivation, and scaffolded support in creating low-risk and positive social environments. • Model and teach students routines necessary for establishing and maintaining positive social environments (e.g., appropriate ways to interact with each other and adults). • Create supportive environments where English learners are encouraged and given many opportunities to use English.
5.3: Use routines to support reading and writing instruction (e.g., time allocation, transitions from one activity to another; discussions, and peer feedback).	• Understand the role of routines in creating and maintaining positive learning environments for reading and writing instruction using traditional print, digital, and online resources. • Create and use routines to support instructional and social goals (e.g., regular steps for sharing and responding to materials read, formats for reporting, and efficient transitions among activities, spaces, and online resources).
5.4: Use a variety of classroom configurations (i.e., whole class, small group, and individual) to differentiate instruction.	• Use evidence-based rationale to make and monitor flexible instructional grouping options for students. • Model and scaffold procedures, so students learn to work effectively in a variety of classroom configurations and activities. • Use various practices to differentiate instruction (e.g., cooperative learning, literature circles, partner work, and research/investigation groups).

Standard 6: Professional Learning and Leadership	Candidates recognize the importance of, demonstrate, and facilitate professional learning and leadership as a career-long effort and responsibility.
Elements	Evidence that demonstrates competence may include, but is not limited to, the following—Middle and High School Reading Classroom Teacher Candidates...
6.1: Demonstrate foundational knowledge of adult learning theories and related research about organizational change, professional development, and school culture.	• Demonstrate an awareness of the factors that influence adult learning, organizational change, professional development, and school culture.
6.2: Display positive dispositions related to their own reading and writing and the teaching of reading and writing, and pursue the development of individual professional knowledge and behaviors.	• Display positive reading and writing behaviors and serve as models for students. • Understand the families' and community's roles in helping students apply reading and writing skills to content learning. • Work with families, colleagues, and the community to support student learning. • Promote student understanding of the value of reading traditional print, digital, and online resources in and out of school. • Identify specific questions and goals about the teaching of reading and writing and plan specific strategies for finding answers to those questions. • Carry out plans and use results for their own professional growth. • Are members of professional organizations related to reading and writing. • Demonstrate effective use of technology for improving student learning.
6.3: Participate in, design, facilitate, lead, and evaluate effective and differentiated professional development programs.	• Recognize the importance of professional development for improving reading and writing in schools. • Participate individually and with colleagues in professional development programs at the school and district levels. • Apply learning from professional development to instructional practices.
6.4: Understand and influence local, state, or national policy decisions.	• Are informed about important professional issues. • Advocate with various groups (e.g., administrators, school boards, and local, state, and federal policymaking bodies) for needed organizational and instructional changes to promote effective literacy instruction.

Reading Specialist/Literacy Coach

Reading Specialists/Literacy Coaches are professionals whose goal is to improve reading achievement in their assigned school or district positions. Their responsibilities and titles often differ based on the context in which they work, and their teaching and educational experiences. Their responsibilities may include teaching, coaching, and leading school reading programs. Reading Specialists/Literacy Coaches may also serve as a resource in reading and writing for educational support personnel, administrators, teachers, and the community, provide professional development based on historical and current literature and research, work collaboratively with other professionals to build and implement reading programs for individuals and groups of students, and serve as advocates for students who struggle with reading. Many of these professionals have a specific focus that further defines their duties, such as serving as a teacher for students experiencing reading difficulties, as a reading or literacy coach, as a coordinator of reading and writing programs at the school or district level, or in several combinations of these roles. Explanations for these roles follow:

• The Reading Specialist/Literacy Coach may have primary responsibility for working with students who struggle with reading and may provide intensive, supplemental instruction to students who struggle with reading at all levels in pre-K–12. Such instruction may be provided either within or outside the students' classrooms. At times, these specialists may provide literacy intervention instruction designed to meet the specific needs of students, or instruction that enables them to meet the requirements of the classroom reading program, or both.

- This specialist may have primary responsibility for supporting teacher learning. These professionals, often known as literacy or reading coaches, provide coaching and other professional development support that enables teachers to think reflectively about improving student learning and implementing various instructional programs and practices. Often, they provide essential leadership for the school's entire literacy program by helping and creating long-term staff development that supports both the development and implementation of a literacy program over months and years. Such work requires these specialists to work with individuals and groups of teachers (e.g., working with grade-level teams and leading study groups).

- These specialists may have primary responsibility for developing, leading, or evaluating the school or district pre-K–12 reading and writing program. These professionals may assume some of the same responsibilities as the specialists who work primarily with teachers but have additional responsibilities that require them to work with systemic change at the school and district levels. These individuals need to have experiences that enable them to work effectively as coordinators and develop and lead effective professional development programs. As coordinators, they may work with special educators, psychologists, and various teachers to develop plans for meeting the needs of all students in the school (e.g., grouping arrangements, assessments, and instructional approaches).

For certification, a Reading Specialist/Literacy Coach Candidate must have the following:

- A valid teaching certificate
- Previous teaching experience
- A master's degree with a concentration in reading and writing education
- Program experiences that build knowledge, skills, and dispositions related to working with students, supporting or coaching teachers, and leading the school reading program
- Typically, the equivalent of 21–27 graduate semester hours in reading, language arts, and related courses: The program must include a supervised practicum experience, typically the equivalent of 6 semester hours.

The supervised practicum experience should require working with students who struggle with reading, as well as collaborative and coaching experiences with teachers. *Note:* It is expected that candidates completing the Reading Specialist/Literacy Coach program will be at a novice or entry level of expertise (see page 68).

Note: The role of the Reading Specialist/Literacy Coach remains as one role because IRA expects to see evidence of both in this candidate: reading specialist and literacy coach.

Standard 1: Foundational Knowledge	Candidates understand the theoretical and evidence-based foundations of reading and writing processes and instruction.
Elements	**Evidence that demonstrates competence may include, but is not limited to, the following—Reading Specialist/Literacy Coach Candidates...**
1.1: Understand major theories and empirical research that describe the cognitive, linguistic, motivational, and sociocultural foundations of reading and writing development, processes, and components, including word recognition, language comprehension, strategic knowledge, and reading–writing connections.	• Interpret major theories of reading and writing processes and development to understand the needs of all readers in diverse contexts. • Analyze classroom environment quality for fostering individual motivation to read and write (e.g., access to print, choice, challenge, and interests). • Demonstrate a critical stance toward the scholarship of the profession. • Read and understand the literature and research about factors that contribute to reading success (e.g., social, cognitive, and physical). • Inform other educators about major theories of reading and writing processes, components, and development with supporting research evidence, including information about the relationship between the culture and native language of English learners as a support system in their learning to read and write in English.
1.2: Understand the historically shared knowledge of the profession and changes over time in the perceptions of reading and writing development, processes, and components.	• Interpret and summarize historically shared knowledge (e.g., instructional strategies and theories) that addresses the needs of all readers. • Inform educators and others about the historically shared knowledge base in reading and writing and its role in reading education.
1.3: Understand the role of professional judgment and practical knowledge for improving all students' reading development and achievement.	• Model fair-mindedness, empathy, and ethical behavior when teaching students and working with other professionals. • Communicate the importance of fair-mindedness, empathy, and ethical behavior in literacy instruction and professional behavior.

Standard 2: Curriculum and Instruction	Candidates use instructional approaches, materials, and an integrated, comprehensive, balanced curriculum to support student learning in reading and writing.
Elements	**Evidence that demonstrates competence may include, but is not limited to, the following—Reading Specialist/Literacy Coach Candidates...**
2.1: Use foundational knowledge to design or implement an integrated, comprehensive, and balanced curriculum.[a]	• Demonstrate an understanding of the research and literature that undergirds the reading and writing curriculum instruction for all pre-K–12 students. • Develop and implement the curriculum to meet the specific needs of students who struggle with reading. • Support teachers and other personnel in the design, implementation, and evaluation of the reading and writing curriculum for all students. • Work with teachers and other personnel in developing a literacy curriculum that has vertical and horizontal alignment across pre-K–12.
2.2: Use appropriate and varied instructional approaches, including those that develop word recognition, language comprehension, strategic knowledge, and reading–writing connections.[b]	• Use instructional approaches supported by literature and research for the following areas: concepts of print, phonemic awareness, phonics, vocabulary, comprehension, fluency, critical thinking, motivation, and writing. • Provide appropriate in-depth instruction for all readers and writers, especially those who struggle with reading and writing. • Support classroom teachers and education support personnel to implement instructional approaches for all students. • As needed, adapt instructional materials and approaches to meet the language-proficiency needs of English learners and students who struggle to learn to read and write.
2.3: Use a wide range of texts (e.g., narrative, expository, and poetry) from traditional print, digital, and online resources.	• Demonstrate knowledge of and a critical stance toward a wide variety of quality traditional print, digital, and online resources. • Support classroom teachers in building and using a quality, accessible classroom library and materials collection that meets the specific needs and abilities of all learners.[c] • Lead collaborative school efforts to evaluate, select, and use a variety of instructional materials to meet the specific needs and abilities of all learners.

[a]Reading specialists may have responsibilities for teaching students who struggle with learning to read and must also be able to support teachers in their efforts to provide effective instruction for all students. [b]McKenna and Stahl (2009) define *reading* as including word recognition, language comprehension, and strategic knowledge (see the Glossary for their definition of *cognitive model of reading*). [c]Reading specialists may provide support through modeling, coteaching, observing, planning, and providing resources.

Standard 3: Assessment and Evaluation	Candidates use a variety of assessment tools and practices to plan and evaluate effective reading and writing instruction.
Elements	**Evidence that demonstrates competence may include, but is not limited to, the following—Reading Specialist/Literacy Coach Candidates…**
3.1: Understand types of assessments and their purposes, strengths, and limitations.	• Demonstrate an understanding of the literature and research related to assessments and their uses and misuses. • Demonstrate an understanding of established purposes for assessing the performance of all readers, including tools for screening, diagnosis, progress monitoring, and measuring outcomes. • Recognize the basic technical adequacy of assessments (e.g., reliability, content, and construct validity). • Explain district and state assessment frameworks, proficiency standards, and student benchmarks.
3.2: Select, develop, administer, and interpret assessments, both traditional print and electronic, for specific purposes.[a]	• Administer and interpret appropriate assessments for students, especially those who struggle with reading and writing. • Collaborate with and provide support to all teachers in the analysis of data, using the assessment results of all students. • Lead schoolwide or larger scale analyses to select assessment tools that provide a systemic framework for assessing the reading, writing, and language growth of all students.
3.3: Use assessment information to plan and evaluate instruction.	• Use multiple data sources to analyze individual readers' performance and to plan instruction and intervention. • Analyze and use assessment data to examine the effectiveness of specific intervention practices and students' responses to instruction. • Lead teachers in analyzing and using classroom, individual, grade-level, or schoolwide assessment data to make instructional decisions. • Plan and evaluate professional development initiatives using assessment data.
3.4: Communicate assessment results and implications to a variety of audiences.	• Analyze and report assessment results to a variety of appropriate audiences for relevant implications, instructional purposes, and accountability. • Demonstrate the ability to communicate results of assessments to various audiences.

[a]Reading specialists may have responsibilities for teaching students who struggle with learning to read and must also be able to support teachers in their efforts to provide effective instruction for all students.

Standard 4: Diversity	Candidates create and engage their students in literacy practices that develop awareness, understanding, respect, and a valuing of differences in our society.
Elements	Evidence that demonstrates competence may include, but is not limited to, the following—Reading Specialist/Literacy Coach Candidates…
4.1: Recognize, understand, and value the forms of diversity that exist in society and their importance in learning to read and write.[a]	• Demonstrate an understanding of the ways in which diversity influences the reading and writing development of students, especially those who struggle with reading and writing. • Assist teachers in developing reading and writing instruction that is responsive to diversity. • Assist teachers in understanding the relationship between first- and second-language acquisition and literacy development. • Engage the school community in conversations about research on diversity and how diversity impacts reading and writing development.
4.2: Use a literacy curriculum and engage in instructional practices that positively impact students' knowledge, beliefs, and engagement with the features of diversity.	• Provide differentiated instruction and instructional materials, including traditional print, digital, and online resources, that capitalize on diversity. • Support classroom teachers in providing differentiated instruction and developing students as agents of their own literacy learning. • Support and lead other educators to recognize their own cultures in order to teach in ways that are responsive to students' diverse backgrounds. • Collaborate with others to build strong home-to-school and school-to-home literacy connections. • Provide support and leadership to educators, parents and guardians, students, and other members of the school community in valuing the contributions of diverse people and traditions to literacy learning.
4.3: Develop and implement strategies to advocate for equity.	• Provide students with linguistic, academic, and cultural experiences that link their communities with the school. • Advocate for change in societal practices and institutional structures that are inherently biased or prejudiced against certain groups. • Demonstrate how issues of inequity and opportunities for social justice activism and resiliency can be incorporated into the literacy curriculum. • Collaborate with teachers, parents and guardians, and administrators to implement policies and instructional practices that promote equity and draw connections between home and community literacy and school literacy.

[a]Reading specialists may have responsibilities for teaching students who struggle with learning to read and must also be able to support teachers in their efforts to provide effective instruction for all students.

Standard 5: Literate Environment	Candidates create a literate environment that fosters reading and writing by integrating foundational knowledge, instructional practices, approaches and methods, curriculum materials, and the appropriate use of assessments.
Elements	Evidence that demonstrates competence may include, but is not limited to, the following—Reading Specialist/Literacy Coach Candidates…
5.1: Design the physical environment to optimize students' use of traditional print, digital, and online resources in reading and writing instruction.	• Arrange instructional areas to provide easy access to books and other instructional materials for a variety of individual, small-group, and whole-class activities and support teachers in doing the same. • Modify the arrangements to accommodate students' changing needs.
5.2: Design a social environment that is low-risk, includes choice, motivation, and scaffolded support to optimize students' opportunities for learning to read and write.[a]	• Create supportive social environments for all students, especially those who struggle with reading and writing. • Model for and support teachers and other professionals in doing the same for all students. • Create supportive environments where English learners are encouraged and given many opportunities to use English.
5.3: Use routines to support reading and writing instruction (e.g., time allocation, transitions from one activity to another; discussions, and peer feedback).	• Understand the role of routines in creating and maintaining positive learning environments for reading and writing instruction using traditional print, digital, and online resources. • Create effective routines for all students, especially those who struggle with reading and writing. • Support teachers in doing the same for all readers.
5.4: Use a variety of classroom configurations (i.e., whole class, small group, and individual) to differentiate instruction.	• Use evidence-based grouping practices to meet the needs of all students, especially those who struggle with reading and writing. • Support teachers in doing the same for all students.

[a]Reading specialists may have responsibilities for teaching students who struggle with learning to read and must also be able to support teachers in their efforts to provide effective instruction for all students.

Standard 6: Professional Learning and Leadership	Candidates recognize the importance of, demonstrate, and facilitate professional learning and leadership as a career-long effort and responsibility.
Elements	**Evidence that demonstrates competence may include, but is not limited to, the following—Reading Specialist/Literacy Coach Candidates…**
6.1: Demonstrate foundational knowledge of adult learning theories and related research about organizational change, professional development, and school culture.	• Use literature and research findings about adult learning, organizational change, professional development, and school culture in working with teachers and other professionals. • Use knowledge of students and teachers to build effective professional development programs. • Use the research base to assist in building an effective, schoolwide professional development program.
6.2: Display positive dispositions related to their own reading and writing and the teaching of reading and writing, and pursue the development of individual professional knowledge and behaviors.[a]	• Articulate the research base related to the connections among teacher dispositions, student learning, and the involvement of parents, guardians, and the community. • Promote the value of reading and writing in and out of school by modeling a positive attitude toward reading and writing with students, colleagues, administrators, and parents and guardians. • Join and participate in professional literacy organizations, symposia, conferences, and workshops. • Demonstrate effective interpersonal, communication, and leadership skills. • Demonstrate effective use of technology for improving student learning.
6.3: Participate in, design, facilitate, lead, and evaluate effective and differentiated professional development programs.	• Collaborate in planning, leading, and evaluating professional development activities for individuals and groups of teachers. Activities may include working individually with teachers (e.g., modeling, coplanning, coteaching, and observing) or with groups (e.g., teacher workshops, group meetings, and online learning). • Demonstrate the ability to hold effective conversations (e.g., for planning and reflective problem solving) with individuals and groups of teachers, work collaboratively with teachers and administrators, and facilitate group meetings. • Support teachers in their efforts to use technology in literacy assessment and instruction.
6.4: Understand and influence local, state, or national policy decisions.	• Demonstrate an understanding of local, state, and national policies that affect reading and writing instruction. • Write or assist in writing proposals that enable schools to obtain additional funding to support literacy efforts. • Promote effective communication and collaboration among stakeholders, including parents and guardians, teachers, administrators, policymakers, and community members. • Advocate with various groups (e.g., administrators, school boards, and local, state, and federal policymaking bodies) for needed organizational and instructional changes to promote effective literacy instruction.

[a]This element deals with positive attitudes not only with colleagues but also with community members, parents and guardians, and so forth.

Teacher Educator

A Teacher Educator is a professional who provides reading teacher preparation to individuals seeking teaching credentials at the undergraduate and graduate levels and candidates seeking advanced graduate credentials in reading. Teacher Educators have a number of other responsibilities as well, such as participating in scholarly activities, including creative works and research studies, and forging university–school partnerships with other education agencies to promote the advancement of literacy. These educators may be responsible for developing programs for preparing reading professionals, including the development of course work and field site experiences, and coordinating or leading such programs. They may also be responsible for supervising and mentoring teacher candidates in the field. These professionals identify and use as role models those classroom teachers who demonstrate exemplary use of instruction, physical arrangements, positive social environments, routines, and grouping practices.

For certification, a Teacher Educator Candidate must have the following:

- A minimum of three years of teaching experience, including the teaching of reading

- A doctorate or exceptional expertise in teaching reading, a license in the fields he or she teaches or supervises, and a record of demonstrated excellence in the teaching of reading

Standard 1: Foundational Knowledge	Candidates understand the theoretical and evidence-based foundations of reading and writing processes and instruction.
Elements	Evidence that demonstrates competence may include, but is not limited to, the following—Teacher Educator Candidates…
1.1: Understand major theories and empirical research that describe the cognitive, linguistic, motivational, and sociocultural foundations of reading and writing development, processes, and components, including word recognition, language comprehension, strategic knowledge, and reading–writing connections.	• Critique major theories of reading and writing processes, components, and development across the life span with supporting research evidence. • Analyze research evidence about language and reading development in all areas, including knowledge about transfer of skills from the primary or home language (L1) to English (L2) as it affects literacy learning for English learners across those components. • Create environments in the university classroom that foster individual motivation to read and write (e.g., access to print, choice, challenge, interests) and teach teachers how to create such environments. • Evaluate knowledge claims of reading research, critique research findings, and generate alternative hypotheses.
1.2: Understand the historically shared knowledge of the profession and changes over time in the perceptions of reading and writing development, processes, and components.	• Analyze historically shared knowledge in reading and writing scholarship and explain its role in an evolving professional knowledge base. • Reevaluate the relevance of historically shared knowledge in meeting traditional print, digital, and online reading education goals.
1.3: Understand the role of professional judgment and practical knowledge for improving all students' reading development and achievement.	• Communicate the importance of fair-mindedness, empathy, and ethical behavior in professional activity.

Standard 2: Curriculum and Instruction	Candidates use instructional approaches, materials, and an integrated, comprehensive, balanced curriculum to support student learning in reading and writing.
Elements	Evidence that demonstrates competence may include, but is not limited to, the following—Teacher Educator Candidates…
2.1: Use foundational knowledge to design or implement an integrated, comprehensive, and balanced curriculum.	• Demonstrate knowledge of and evaluate reading and writing curriculum (PreK–12). • Convey knowledge and understanding of curriculum to candidates and reading professionals. • Provide opportunities for candidates and reading professionals to develop an integrated, comprehensive, and balanced curriculum.
2.2: Use appropriate and varied instructional approaches, including those that develop word recognition, language comprehension, strategic knowledge, and reading–writing connections.	• Provide opportunities for preservice teachers and other reading professionals to understand conceptual underpinnings and evidence based rationales of instructional approaches. • Provide opportunities for preservice teachers and other reading professionals to select, implement, and evaluate instructional approaches based on knowledge of students' needs and interests, and theory-based knowledge.
2.3: Use a wide range of texts (e.g., narrative, expository, and poetry) from traditional print, digital, and online resources.	• Provide opportunities for preservice teachers and other reading professionals to review and critique a wide variety of quality traditional print, digital, and online resources. • Provide opportunities for preservice teachers and other reading professionals to establish criteria for selecting quality traditional print, digital, and online resources for all students, including English learners.

Standard 3: Assessment and Evaluation	Candidates use a variety of assessment tools and practices to plan and evaluate effective reading and writing instruction.
Elements	Evidence that demonstrates competence may include, but is not limited to, the following—Teacher Educator Candidates…
3.1: Understand types of assessments and their purposes, strengths, and limitations.	• Prepare preservice teachers and other reading professionals to select, analyze, and use assessment tools based on established purposes. • Analyze and critique a range of assessment tools based on established purposes. • Contribute to the scholarly dialogue about assessment. • Read and understand the literature and research related to assessments, their use and misuse.
3.2: Select, develop, administer, and interpret assessments, both traditional print and electronic, for specific purposes.	• Prepare preservice teachers and other reading professionals to administer and interpret assessments for selected purposes. • Analyze and critique a range of diagnostic assessment tools for students in need of reading and writing assistance.
3.3: Use assessment information to plan and evaluate instruction.	• Prepare preservice teachers and other reading professionals to examine the role of assessment in the delivery of effective reading instruction. • Prepare preservice teachers and other reading professionals to adjust instruction based on ongoing assessment.
3.4: Communicate assessment results and implications to a variety of audiences.	• Prepare and coach preservice teachers and other reading professionals to communicate assessment results to various audiences in ways that lead to improved instruction.

Standard 4: Diversity	Candidates create and engage their students in literacy practices that develop awareness, understanding, respect, and a valuing of differences in our society.
Elements	Evidence that demonstrates competence may include, but is not limited to, the following—Teacher Educator Candidates…
4.1: Recognize, understand, and value the forms of diversity that exist in society and their importance in learning to read and write.	• Demonstrate an understanding of current theoretical perspectives and empirical evidence related to diversity and reading and writing development and prepare preservice teachers and other reading professionals to understand the relationship between first and second language acquisition and literacy development.
4.2: Use a literacy curriculum and engage in instructional practices that positively impact students' knowledge, beliefs, and engagement with the features of diversity.	• Engage preservice teachers and other reading professionals in multiple experiences and settings to strengthen their understandings about the ways that multiple identities of students intersect with curriculum orientations, literacy instruction, and student agency. • Collaborate with preservice teachers and other reading professionals to identify and advocate for forms of pedagogy, curriculum orientations, and professional development practices that focus on students' diversity. • Provide opportunities for preservice teachers and other reading professionals to reflect on and evaluate literacy-related experiences aimed at providing responsive instruction that honors students' diversity.
4.3: Develop and implement strategies to advocate for equity.	• Prepare, coach, and collaborate with preservice teachers and other reading professionals to respond to literacy practices (both in and outside school) that are inequitable and unfair and replace them with practices that are equitable and fair. • Provide and promote experiences for reading professionals that reflect and/or nurture the ideas of tolerance and equity.

Standard 5: Literate Environment	Candidates create a literate environment that fosters reading and writing by integrating foundational knowledge, instructional practices, approaches and methods, curriculum materials, and the appropriate use of assessments.
Elements	**Evidence that demonstrates competence may include, but is not limited to, the following—Teacher Educator Candidates…**
5.1: Design the physical environment to optimize students' use of traditional print, digital, and online resources in reading and writing instruction.	• Arrange the university classroom in ways that facilitate understanding the role of the physical environment in reading and writing instruction.
5.2: Design a social environment that is low-risk, includes choice, motivation, and scaffolded support to optimize students' opportunities for learning to read and write.	• Create a positive social environment in the higher education classroom. • Provide opportunities to create positive social environments. • Collaborate with candidates, colleagues, teachers, and other professionals to create positive social environments at the university and in schools, including supportive environment where English learners are given many opportunities to use English.
5.3: Use routines to support reading and writing instruction (e.g., time allocation, transitions from one activity to another; discussions, and peer feedback).	• Create effective classroom routines in the higher education classroom. • Provide opportunities for candidates and reading professionals to create and use classroom routines. • Collaborate with colleagues, teachers, and other professionals to create positive social environments that incorporate the use of technology at the university and in schools.
5.4: Use a variety of classroom configurations (i.e., whole class, small group, and individual) to differentiate instruction.	• Prepare reading professionals to use evidence-based instructional grouping options for students. • Provide evidenced-based information supporting different models of classroom organization and relative benefits and limitations.

Standard 6: Professional Learning and Leadership	Candidates recognize the importance of, demonstrate, and facilitate professional learning and leadership as a career-long effort and responsibility.
Elements	**Evidence that demonstrates competence may include, but is not limited to, the following—Teacher Educator Candidates…**
6.1: Demonstrate foundational knowledge of adult learning theories and related research about organizational change, professional development, and school culture.	• Examine and critique the literature on organizational change, adult learning, professional development, and school culture. • Have knowledge of interinstitutional collaboration and cooperation.
6.2: Display positive dispositions related to their own reading and writing and the teaching of reading and writing, and pursue the development of individual professional knowledge and behaviors.	• Promote a positive and ethical learning environment with an emphasis on collaboration and respect that responds to students, families, teachers, and communities. • Demonstrate strong interpersonal and communication skills as evident in interactions with all stakeholders. • Provide opportunities for candidates and reading professionals to share their own reading and writing. • Conduct research and communicate results for appropriate purposes and audiences. • Join and regularly participate in professional literacy organizations, conferences, symposia, and workshops. • Prepare and coach candidates and reading professionals to use various forms of research to inform practice.
6.3: Participate in, design, facilitate, lead, and evaluate effective and differentiated professional development programs.	• Know and critique the research on professional development. • Prepare and coach reading professionals to collaboratively plan, lead, and evaluate professional development activities at the grade, school, district, community, and state levels. • Participate in professional development at the national level through attendance and/or presentation at professional meetings, conferences, or symposia.
6.4: Understand and influence local, state, or national policy decisions.	• Read and critique the literature about state and federal initiatives having implications for reading and writing instruction. • Provide opportunities for candidates and reading professionals to learn about these initiatives and their implications for reading and writing instruction. • Advocate for needed organizational and instructional changes to promote effective literacy instruction.

Administrator

The Administrator (e.g., principal, supervisor of instruction and curriculum, or superintendent) is a professional with the responsibility of administering school and district units. These professionals have a number of responsibilities, including supporting reading professionals as they plan, implement, and evaluate effective reading instruction, and providing necessary resources (i.e., time, personnel, and materials) for effective reading instruction.

For certification, an Administrator Candidate must have the following:

- A master's degree with a concentration in instructional leadership and administration

- Course work in reading and reading-related areas

Standard 1: Foundational Knowledge	Candidates understand the theoretical and evidence-based foundations of reading and writing processes and instruction.
Elements	Evidence that demonstrates competence may include, but is not limited to, the following—Administrator Candidates…
1.1: Understand major theories and empirical research that describe the cognitive, linguistic, motivational, and sociocultural foundations of reading and writing development, processes, and components, including word recognition, language comprehension, strategic knowledge, and reading–writing connections.	• Recognize major theories and research evidence related to reading and writing development and instruction. • Identify the specific reading and writing expectations of PreK-12 students as described in national and state standards. • Plan for environments that support individual motivation to read and write (e.g., access to print, choice, challenge, interests). • Value the scholarship of the reading profession and seek to understand the theoretical knowledge base in relation to one's administrative charge.
1.2: Understand the historically shared knowledge of the profession and changes over time in the perceptions of reading and writing development, processes, and components.	• Identify evidence-based instructional approaches, techniques and procedures relevant to the reading and writing demands of PreK-12 instruction. • Examine critically practices contributing to applied knowledge of reading education.
1.3: Understand the role of professional judgment and practical knowledge for improving all students' reading development and achievement.	• Encourage reading professionals to show fair-mindedness, empathy, and ethical behavior in teaching students and working with other professionals. • Model such behaviors in work with professional staff.

Standard 2: Curriculum and Instruction	Candidates use instructional approaches, materials, and an integrated, comprehensive, balanced curriculum to support student learning in reading and writing.
Elements	Evidence that demonstrates competence may include, but is not limited to, the following—Administrator Candidates…
2.1: Use foundational knowledge to design or implement an integrated, comprehensive, and balanced curriculum.	• Monitor instruction to determine that standards are met. • Provide opportunities for review and alignment of curriculum with standards.
2.2: Use appropriate and varied instructional approaches, including those that develop word recognition, language comprehension, strategic knowledge, and reading–writing connections.	• Provide ongoing, integrated professional development opportunities that allow the demonstration and of modeling of practical and evidence-based approaches. • Provide opportunities for teachers' self-reflection and interaction with peers. • Provide professional materials and encourage study/discussion groups.
2.3: Use a wide range of texts (e.g., narrative, expository, and poetry) from traditional print, digital, and online resources.	• Demonstrate a critical stance towards instructional materials used for reading and writing instruction. • Provide opportunities for demonstrations, evaluations, and usage of a wide range of instructional materials that support student learning.

Standard 3: Assessment and Evaluation	Candidates use a variety of assessment tools and practices to plan and evaluate effective reading and writing instruction.
Elements	Evidence that demonstrates competence may include, but is not limited to, the following—Administrator Candidates…
3.1: Understand types of assessments and their purposes, strengths, and limitations.	• Demonstrate an understanding of literature and research related to assessments, their uses and misuses. • Explain district and state assessment frameworks, proficiency standards, and student benchmarks. • Explain large scale assessment designs, state and district assessment frameworks, proficiency standards, and benchmarks.
3.2: Select, develop, administer, and interpret assessments, both traditional print and electronic, for specific purposes.	• Provide time and fiscal resources to facilitate assessment. • Support the development of sound assessment design across classrooms.
3.3: Use assessment information to plan and evaluate instruction.	• Use student data to facilitate curricular, grouping, literacy staffing pattern decisions within schools and across schools and within the district.
3.4: Communicate assessment results and implications to a variety of audiences.	• Analyze and communicate federal, state, and local assessment results to internal staff and external partners, e.g., community members, policymakers, and other stakeholders. • Analyze and communicate literacy performance goals as identified in federal and state law and implications of those goals on literacy curriculum, instruction, and assessment.

Standard 4: Diversity	Candidates create and engage their students in literacy practices that develop awareness, understanding, respect, and a valuing of differences in our society.
Elements	Evidence that demonstrates competence may include, but is not limited to, the following—Administrator Candidates…
4.1: Recognize, understand, and value the forms of diversity that exist in society and their importance in learning to read and write.	• Examine, evaluate and articulate how students' diversity informs pedagogy, selection of curricula, and professional development practices. • Support and collaborate with teachers, parents or guardians, and community members to provide experiences responsive to students' diverse needs. • Plan for and sustain a school culture that is supportive of diversity that exists among teachers and students.
4.2: Use a literacy curriculum and engage in instructional practices that positively impact students' knowledge, beliefs, and engagement with the features of diversity.	• Examine, evaluate, and articulate how instructional programs, curriculum materials, and assessment practices impact the literacy outcomes of diverse students. • Identify human and material resources to effectively shape learning environments that are responsive to the various features of student diversity.
4.3: Develop and implement strategies to advocate for equity.	• Ensure that school contexts, structures, and teachers' professional practices are supportive of, responsive to and respectful of teachers', students', and parents' or guardians' diversity. • Collaborate with all stakeholders to mobilize efforts to be responsive to students' diversity.

Standard 5: Literate Environment	Candidates create a literate environment that fosters reading and writing by integrating foundational knowledge, instructional practices, approaches and methods, curriculum materials, and the appropriate use of assessments.
Elements	**Evidence that demonstrates competence may include, but is not limited to, the following—Administrator Candidates…**
5.1: Design the physical environment to optimize students' use of traditional print, digital, and online resources in reading and writing instruction.	• Provide resources and encourage flexibility in creating the physical environment.
5.2: Design a social environment that is low-risk, includes choice, motivation, and scaffolded support to optimize students' opportunities for learning to read and write.	• Foster a climate in the school that consistently demands positive social interactions from adults and students.
5.3: Use routines to support reading and writing instruction (e.g., time allocation, transitions from one activity to another; discussions, and peer feedback).	• Understand how classroom routines can facilitate reading and writing instruction. • Provide a school level infrastructure that supports the use of effective classroom routines.
5.4: Use a variety of classroom configurations (i.e., whole class, small group, and individual) to differentiate instruction.	• Provide resources and encourage flexibility in differentiating instruction. • Recruit community members as mentors, tutors, volunteers, and resource-providers to support literacy growth at the school.

Standard 6: Professional Learning and Leadership	Candidates recognize the importance of, demonstrate, and facilitate professional learning and leadership as a career-long effort and responsibility.
Elements	**Evidence that demonstrates competence may include, but is not limited to, the following—Administrator Candidates…**
6.1: Demonstrate foundational knowledge of adult learning theories and related research about organizational change, professional development, and school culture.	• Connect foundational knowledge associated with educational leadership to the organizational and instructional knowledge required to implement an effective schoolwide reading program. • Apply knowledge from a variety of disciplines to promote a positive school culture and climate for students and adults.
6.2: Display positive dispositions related to their own reading and writing and the teaching of reading and writing, and pursue the development of individual professional knowledge and behaviors.	• Ensure a positive and ethical learning context for reading that respects students, families, teachers, colleagues, and communities. • Foster community involvement in schoolwide literacy initiatives. • Encourage and support teachers and reading professionals to develop their knowledge, skills, and dispositions. • Provide leadership by participating in ongoing professional development with staff and others in leadership positions. • Encourage use of technology among teachers and other personnel for their own learning and for improving student learning.
6.3: Participate in, design, facilitate, lead, and evaluate effective and differentiated professional development programs.	• Work collaboratively with school staff to plan, implement, and evaluate sustained professional development programs to meet established needs, grade/discipline, or individual levels. • Provide varied professional development opportunities for those having responsibility for student learning.
6.4: Understand and influence local, state, or national policy decisions.	• Promote effective communication and collaboration among parents or guardians, community, and school staff. • Understand the importance of hiring highly qualified literacy personnel, providing clear role descriptions for literacy positions, and supporting individuals in those positions. • Advocate at local, state, and federal levels for needed organizational and instructional changes to promote effective literacy instruction.

PART 3

Research Base for Standards

Reading, reading instruction, and teacher preparation for reading instruction are among the most studied topics in educational research. Because of the sheer volume of the work, researchers, publishers, and the U.S. Department of Education have devoted significant resources to research syntheses that summarize historical and current research findings. Rather than providing another such synthesis, *Standards 2010* provides a sampling of well-respected extant syntheses. In this section, we provide a complete bibliographic reference and a short commentary that highlights the relevance of the particular synthesis to each of the six professional Standards.

In addition, IRA is publishing the second edition of *Preparing Reading Professionals*, which is a collection of articles and book chapters that includes both research and descriptions of practice that will help users of *Standards 2010* add depth and detail to their understandings of each standard.

The Handbooks of Reading Research

- Pearson, P.D., Barr, R., Kamil, M.L., & Mosenthal, P. (Eds.). (1984). *Handbook of reading research* (Vol. 1). White Plains, NY: Longman.

- Barr, R., Kamil, M.L., Mosenthal, P., & Pearson, P.D. (Eds.). (1991). *Handbook of reading research* (Vol. 2). White Plains, NY: Longman.

- Kamil, M.L., Mosenthal, P.B., Pearson, P.D., & Barr, R. (Eds.). (2000). *Handbook of reading research* (Vol. 3). Mahwah, NJ: Erlbaum.

The Handbooks of Reading Research were published at approximately decade intervals. These handbooks are voluminous and a treasure trove of research syntheses. Among the three volumes, there are chapters relevant to all six Standards. Scholars should be intimately acquainted with all three books; the volumes are also relevant to the work of those using *Standards 2010*.

Research Syntheses

- Biancarosa, G., & Snow, C.E. (2006). *Reading next: A vision for action and research in middle and high school literacy* (2nd ed.). Washington, DC: Alliance for Excellent Education.

Reading Next is a report that combines current research with well-crafted strategies for turning that research into practice. Informed by some of the nation's leading researchers, this book charts an immediate route to improving adolescent literacy. The authors outline 15 key elements of an effective adolescent literacy intervention and call on public and private stakeholders to invest in the literacy of middle and high school students today, while simultaneously building the knowledge base. *Standards 2010* users will find *Reading Next* useful, especially in relation to Standard 2 (Curriculum and Instruction) and Standard 3 (Assessment and Evaluation).

- Borko, H. (2004). Professional development and teacher learning: Mapping the terrain. *Educational Researcher, 33*(8), 3–15.

This article maps the research on teacher professional development by providing an overview of what we have learned as a field about effective professional development programs and their impact on teacher learning. Borko suggests some important directions and strategies for extending our knowledge into a new territory of questions not yet explored.

- Cowen, J.E. (2003). *A balanced approach to beginning reading instruction: A synthesis of six major U.S. research studies.* Newark, DE: International Reading Association.

Particularly relevant to Standard 1 (Foundational Knowledge), this book summarizes and evaluates six major government-funded research studies. Anyone with expertise in reading and reading instruction should be familiar with these seminal studies.

- Farstrup, A.E., & Samuels, S.J. (Eds.). (2002). *What research has to say about reading instruction* (3rd ed.). Newark, DE: International Reading Association.

This volume contains 17 chapters, each devoted to summarizing the research on a particular topic, and is particularly useful for understanding Standard 2 (Curriculum and Instruction), because it provides research evidence for the teaching and learning of specific reading skills and strategies. Many of the chapters address the teaching of specific aspects of reading (e.g., phonics, phonemic awareness, vocabulary, fluency, and reading comprehension). Two chapters address Standard 3 (Assessment and Evaluation), and several chapters summarize research related to Standard 4 (Diversity).

- Pressley, M. (2001). Effective beginning reading instruction. *Journal of Literacy Research, 34*(2), 165–188.

This review critiques the findings of the National Reading Panel, highlights additional findings supported by rigorous research, and is particularly useful for Standard 2 (Curriculum and Instruction) and Standard 5 (Literate Environment). Pressley addresses the importance of classroom practices and routines that benefit literacy achievement. Effective reading instruction occurs over the years and changes with the developmental level of the child, and these dynamics are not captured by the Panel's emphases on discrete skills appropriate only to particular developmental levels. Effective instruction is a balance and blending of skills teaching and holistic literature and writing experiences.

- Risko, V.J., Roller, C.M., Cummins, C., Bean, R.M., Block, C.C., Anders, P.L., et al. (2008). A critical analysis of research on reading teacher education. *Reading Research Quarterly, 43*(3), 252–288.

This article is particularly useful for background related to Standard 6 (Professional Learning and Leadership). Risko et al. summarize 82 studies and include findings that indicate that reading teacher preparation programs have been relatively successful in recent years in changing prospective teachers' knowledge and beliefs; a smaller number of studies document that pedagogical knowledge has influenced actual teaching practice under certain conditions. The authors suggest that university teaching practices that benefit learning of pedagogical knowledge and skills tend to provide explicit explanation and examples, demonstrations of practices, and opportunities for guided practice of teaching practices in practicum settings with pupils.

- Ruddell, R.B., & Unrau, N.J. (Eds.). (2004). *Theoretical models and processes of reading* (5th ed.). Newark, DE: International Reading Association.

Theoretical Models and Processes of Reading is a periodic volume that reprints seminal articles related to reading and reading instruction. Its opening section is useful for understanding Standard 1 (Foundational Knowledge), because it gives a historical perspective on the teaching of reading and on reading research. Section 2 includes eight chapters devoted to language and cognition in sociocultural contexts. Ruddell and Unrau also included a section on models of reading and writing processes. The volume is also relevant to Standard 2 (Curriculum and Instruction), because it includes many chapters devoted to specific instructional practices about early reading and the development of skilled reading in middle and high school students.

- Sailors, M., & Hoffman, J. (2010). The text environment and learning to read: Windows and mirrors shaping literate lives. In D.Wyse, R. Andrews, & J. Hoffman (Eds.), *The Routledge international handbook of English, language and literacy teaching* (pp. 294–304). New York: Routledge.

This review is particularly relevant to Standard 5 (Literate Environment). Sailors and Hoffman have adopted the metaphor of mirrors and windows to frame their analysis of theory, research, practice, and reform as related to the literacy environment created in the classroom. They argue that the text environment mediates the literacy lives of learners, as they may or may not engage with texts in and out of school. They also argue that it is helpful to examine the uses of literacy from multiple theoretical frames, including the psychological, sociopsychological, social practice, critical, and aesthetic. The gap is still great in terms of schools realizing the potential for the literacy environment.

- Slavin, R.E. (1987). Ability grouping and student achievement in elementary schools: A best-evidence synthesis. *Review of Educational Research*, 57(3), 293–336.

Although somewhat dated, this is an excellent review of the literature on grouping practices in reading instruction and is particularly relevant to Standard 5 (Literate Environment). Slavin reviewed the effects of between- and within-class ability grouping on the achievement of elementary school students. Overall, evidence does not support assignment of students to self-contained classes according to ability, but grouping plans involving cross-grade assignment for selected subjects can increase student achievement. Research particularly supports the Joplin Plan, cross-grade ability grouping for reading only. Analysis of effects of alternative grouping methods suggests that ability grouping is maximally effective when done for only one or two subjects (with students remaining in heterogeneous classes most of the day), when it greatly reduces student heterogeneity in a specific skill, when group assignments are frequently reassessed, and when teachers vary the level and pace of instruction according to student needs.

- York-Barr, J., & Duke, K. (2004). What do we know about teacher leadership? Findings from two decades of scholarship. *Review of Educational Research*, *74*(3), 255–316.

This article reviews the research literature about professional development and is specifically focused on Standard 6 (Professional Learning and Leadership). The review of the empirical literature revealed numerous small-scale, qualitative studies that describe dimensions of teacher leadership practice, teacher leader characteristics, and conditions that promote and offer a conceptual framework to guide future inquiry.

Government-Sponsored Reports

- Snow, C.E., Burns, M.S., & Griffin, P. (Eds.). (1998). *Preventing reading difficulties in young children*. Washington, DC: National Academy Press.

This was the first of the series of U.S. government–funded reports related to reading instruction. This report focused on pre-K through third grade and is an excellent source for descriptions of reading skills and behaviors at each level. It is not a research synthesis, because it does not approach the task by identifying research studies and then synthesizing. Instead, the Committee on the Prevention of Reading Difficulties in Young Children used the knowledge of its distinguished panel to guide findings and recommendations. This report is most useful in relation to Standard 2 (Curriculum and Instruction) and Standard 3 (Assessment and Evaluation), at the early reading level.

- National Institute of Child Health and Human Development. (2000). *Report of the National Reading Panel. Teaching children to read: An evidence-based assessment of the scientific research literature on reading and its implications for reading instruction* (NIH Publication No. 00-4769). Washington, DC: U.S. Government Printing Office.

This document is usually referred to as the National Reading Panel Report and is particularly useful for understanding Standard 2 (Curriculum and Instruction). It specifically addresses the teaching and learning of phonemic awareness, phonics, vocabulary, fluency, and comprehension strategies and is an excellent summary of the experimental and quasi-experimental studies on these topics that were completed by the late 1990s.

- National Early Literacy Panel. (2008). *Developing early literacy: Report of the National Early Literacy Panel*. Washington, DC: National Institute for Literacy.

This report focused on identifying the early literacy skills that predict later achievement in reading and then identifying instructional practices that research indicates improves those early skills. It is particularly useful for Standard 2 (Curriculum and Instruction), because its major focus is on instructional practices. As the title indicates, the report focuses only on early literacy and will be of most interest to those involved with pre-K–2 reading.

- August, D., & Shanahan, T. (Eds.). (2006). *Developing literacy in second-language learners: Report of the National Literacy Panel on Language-Minority Children and Youth*. Mahwah, NJ: Erlbaum; Washington, DC: Center for Applied Linguistics.

This volume reports the findings of the National Literacy Panel on Language-Minority Children and Youth. The formal charge to the panel—a distinguished group of expert researchers in reading, language, bilingualism, research methods, and education—was to identify, assess, and synthesize research on the education of language-minority children and youth with respect to their attainment of literacy. This volume is particularly useful in relation to Standard 4 (Diversity), as it focuses specifically on instructional methods for children learning English as a second language.

- Yoon, K.S., Duncan, T., Lee, S.W., Scarloss, B., & Shapley, K.L. (2007). *Reviewing the evidence on how teacher professional development affects student achievement* (Issues and Answers Report, REL 2007–No. 033). Washington, DC: Regional Educational Laboratory Southwest, National Center for Education Evaluation and Regional Assistance, Institute of Education Sciences, U.S. Department of Education. Retrieved May 18, 2010, from ies.ed.gov/ncee/edlabs/projects/project.asp?ProjectID = 70

This report addresses Standard 6 (Professional Learning and Leadership). The researchers found that teachers who receive substantial professional development—an average of 49 hours in the nine rigorous studies reviewed—can boost their students' achievement by about 21 percentile points; however, it was based on only nine rigorous studies. Although more than 1,300 studies were identified as having potentially addressed the effect of teacher professional development on student achievement in three key content areas, only nine met the What Works Clearinghouse evidence standards, attesting to the paucity of rigorous studies that directly examine this link.

Evidence Summary of the Standards' Research Base

The publications in the following table are presented in the order they were discussed in this section.

Publication	Standards					
	1	2	3	4	5	6
Pearson, Barr, Kamil, & Mosenthal (1984)	X	X	X	X	X	X
Barr, Kamil, Mosenthal, & Pearson (1991)	X	X	X	X	X	X
Kamil, Mosenthal, Pearson, & Barr (2000)	X	X	X	X	X	X
Biancarosa & Snow (2006)	X	X	X	X	X	X
Borko (2004)						X
Cowen (2003)	X					
Farstrup & Samuels (2002)	X	X	X	X	X	X
Pressley (2001)	X	X			X	
Risko et. al. (2008)						X
Ruddell & Unrau (2004)	X	X	X	X	X	X
Sailors & Hoffman (2010)		X			X	
Slavin (1987)					X	
York-Barr & Duke (2004)						X
Snow, Burns, & Griffin (1998)	X	X	X			
National Institute of Child Health and Human Development (2000)	X	X				X
National Early Literacy Panel (2008)	X	X				
August & Shanahan (2006)	X	X	X	X	X	
Yoon, Duncan, Lee, Scarloss, & Shapley (2007)						X

PART 4

Issues in Reading Education That Affected Standards Development

The Standards 2010 Committee deliberated about several important educational issues that affected the development and content of *Standards 2010*. In this section, we provide an explanation of the thinking that informed the decision making of the Committee. Issues discussed include the Reading Specialist/Literacy Coach role, English learners, Response to Intervention, the use of the terms *all readers* and *struggling readers*, and specificity in professional standards.

Reading Specialist/Literacy Coach Roles

Committee members had many discussions about how to address the roles of the Reading Specialist/Literacy Coach. The reading specialist has a long history in schools, often assuming multiple roles, such as working with struggling readers, assessing students with reading difficulties, and serving as a literacy leader by coordinating literacy efforts, serving as a resource to teachers, assisting in the development of the curriculum or the selection of materials, and helping teachers modify instruction to meet the needs of students in the school. In other words, reading specialists have often been assigned or undertaken a role similar to that of a literacy coach.

Recently, however, the new role of literacy coach has been introduced into schools. The major function of these educators is to provide support to teachers in their instructional efforts and specifically to help reading professionals provide the differentiated instruction necessary to meet the needs of all students in the classroom. Often, reading specialists have been asked to serve as literacy coaches, or districts interested in hiring literacy coaches have, in their job description, indicated that candidates for the coach position must have a reading specialist certificate. However, in some cases, individuals who do not have such certification have been hired, sometimes because of the difficulty in finding qualified individuals for the position (see Frost & Bean [2006] and IRA's [2004] position statement on reading coaches).

What is evident is that the distinguishing differences between a reading specialist and a literacy coach are not clearly delineated. Therefore, the Standards 2010 Committee debated the wisdom of developing a separate set of competencies for literacy coaches alone, in addition to the set for the reading specialist. In the end, the Committee decided to maintain the Reading Specialist/Literacy Coach role as is for the following reasons.

First, as defined in the IRA (2000) position statement on the role of the reading specialist, individuals in that role have a dual responsibility: working with struggling readers and supporting the efforts of classroom teachers.

Therefore, reading specialists need to have the leadership skills, similar to those needed by literacy coaches, that enable them to support and provide leadership to teachers, even though their major responsibility may be working with struggling readers. With the many efforts to provide appropriate instruction for all students in the classroom, this leadership role is an important one for reading specialists. Further, by keeping the two roles as one, we felt that we would be able to promote the importance of reading specialist certification as an important credential for literacy coaches. Finally, the term *literacy coach* is a somewhat new title that has not stood the test of time, and it was our hope that by keeping the two roles as one, we would provide local educational agencies with the flexibility they needed when thinking about how reading specialists might function in their schools.

To provide guidance to those institutions with reading specialist certification programs, we are more specific in *Standards 2010* about the coaching competencies needed by candidates in the program. In describing the possible evidence for the Reading Specialist/Literacy Coach Candidate, we follow, when appropriate, a similar format across standards: The candidate can *do*, can *support* (teachers), and can *lead*. This breakdown supports the notion that reading specialists must, for example, be able to administer and interpret various assessment instruments, support teachers in administering and interpreting assessment instruments, and lead professional development sessions that provide teachers with the knowledge and understanding of various assessments and how they can be used.

We acknowledge that when candidates complete a reading specialist/ literacy coach program, they are at the novice level; that is, they have entry skills for the position. We also acknowledge that candidates for a position that emphasizes the coaching role should have the experiential background that would enable them to gain the trust and establish the credibility necessary to support the work of teachers. Specifically, those being employed for coaching positions should have taught in the classroom, especially at the level (i.e., elementary, middle, or high school) at which they are going to coach. Further, experiences in working with struggling readers would be important, as these professionals will be helping teachers address the needs of students who experience difficulty with reading and writing (see IRA [2004]).

Although the Standards 2010 Committee made the decision to maintain the Reading Specialist/Literacy Coach designation, we believe the next seven years, after which time there will most likely be another revision of the Standards, will bring new knowledge and understanding of the literacy coaching role. At that time, the research evidence about the coaching role should provide useful information to those with the responsibility of revising the Standards, particularly about how to represent the Reading Specialist/ Literacy Coach role.

Response to Intervention

During Committee deliberations and in the feedback received by the field, there were questions about how the Standards would address the Individuals With Disabilities Education Act of 2004, which encourages schools to use an approach different from the traditional discrepancy one for identifying students with learning difficulties and also supports early intervention to reduce the number of students qualifying for special education. This federal initiative suggests that school personnel use formal and informal assessment results to decide whether instruction is effective and, if not, to make modifications (e.g., providing additional time, changing approaches, reducing size of group, or providing more specialized help). This initiative requires collaboration among classroom teachers, reading specialists/literacy coaches, and special educators, with each professional contributing ideas for how to make these instructional adjustments.

Although not mentioning Response to Intervention specifically, *Standards 2010* is based on the notion that reading personnel must understand how to use assessment tools to understand the needs of students and also have knowledge and understanding of how to modify instruction to meet student needs. In that sense, the users of *Standards 2010* will find references throughout the document to the need for candidates to be able to identify students' responses to the instruction they are receiving and to make appropriate adaptations. We refer users to the work of the IRA (2009) Response to Intervention Commission, which has developed guidelines for the development of such programs in schools.

English Learners

The Standards 2010 Committee is grateful to the subcommittee on language diversity, chaired by MaryEllen Vogt, for its comments about English learners and the need for the Standards to address the needs of these students. As stated by Vogt,

> Addressing the academic and language development needs of students whose home language differs from the language of instruction requires that curriculum and instruction are adapted appropriately to meet English learners' distinct needs. This involves specific knowledge and an additional set of skills that educators at all levels must develop. Also, it is incorrect to group English learners with struggling readers. Some English learners *are* struggling readers, in both their first and second language. Other English learners are very competent readers in their first language, but they struggle to read in English because of their particular level of English proficiency. The number of English learners in schools has increased dramatically since 2003 and these students are not monolithically uniform. Certainly, institutions preparing reading professionals have a responsibility to provide knowledge and experiences that will prepare its candidates to effectively teach language minority students. (personal communication, February 2009)

Therefore, in several elements and indicators, there are specific references to English learners; at the same time, whenever there is mention of the need to provide for *all* readers and writers, we encourage users of *Standards 2010* to recognize the importance of providing experiences that address the differing needs of English learners.

Defining the Terms *All Students* and *Struggling Readers*

In the Glossary, *all students* (and *all readers*) is defined as including all students, from those who are advanced and proficient or gifted and talented, as well as those who may experience difficulty with reading and writing, such as English learners, students with disabilities, racially and ethnically diverse students, and mentally disabled students. There is a basic assumption that reading professionals must be able to address the instructional needs of the entire range of readers.

The term *struggling readers* also generated many questions and comments from the Committee. For example, as mentioned previously, not all English learners have difficulty learning to read and write; neither do all students who are racially and ethnically diverse. *Standards 2010* uses the language "students who struggle with reading and writing" by design to include any student experiencing difficulty in learning to read and write. Our assumption is that the term *struggling readers* describes behavior and does not imply any specific causes or identify students as belonging to a specific category, such as having a particular learning disability.

Two of the most critical assumptions underlying *Standards 2010* is that learning to read and write is complex, and readers and writers are complex as well. To be successful, instruction must be differentiated to meet the needs of individual children and for children sharing a variety of group characteristics. Throughout *Standards 2010*, you will find language related to differentiated instruction. Several examples in elements follow:

> 1.3: Understand the role of professional judgment and practical knowledge for improving all students' reading development and achievement.
>
> 3.3: Use assessment information to plan and evaluate instruction.
>
> 5.4: Use a variety of classroom configurations (i.e., whole class, small group, and individual) to differentiate instruction.

The assumption of *Standards 2010* is that all children are entitled to receive instruction that is effectively adapted to meet their particular needs regardless of the factors that led to those needs. *Standards 2010* is committed to developing reading professionals who can deliver appropriately differentiated instruction to meet the needs of all students.

Another issue related to students who struggle with reading and writing relates to the Reading Specialist/Literacy Coach role. There were comments during the public review that indicated that the Reading Specialist/Literacy Coach role should focus on all readers not just struggling readers. The Standards 2010 Committee agrees with this notion. Reading Specialists/ Literacy Coaches may have responsibility for working directly with students who struggle with reading by serving as their teacher. However, these professionals are also responsible for the instruction of all students in their leadership and coaching roles and work with teachers and other professionals to assure that all children are receiving optimal instruction.

Specificity of the Standards

Some comments were made about whether the Standards were specific enough to help users evaluate, develop, and implement programs. A few questioned whether there was enough attention to a specific topic (e.g., phonics or critical thinking). Specificity is an issue that frequently surfaces during standards development efforts. On one hand, professionals want to have a standards document that provides an overview of the knowledge and organizing principles of a field. On the other hand, they also want it to describe exactly what teachers should know and be able to do. *Standards 2010* is intended to accomplish the former objective and does not attempt to provide a complete curriculum for the development of the seven categories of reading professionals.

Standards 2010, however, is comprehensive and provides users with information essential for program development and review. For example, in element 1.1 of Standard 1 (Foundational Knowledge), the language for the Pre-K and Elementary Classroom Teacher Candidate is specific, as evidenced in the following example:

Standard 1: Foundational Knowledge	Candidates understand the theoretical and evidence-based foundations of reading and writing processes and instruction.
Elements	Evidence that demonstrates competence may include, but is not limited to, the following—Pre-K and Elementary Classroom Teacher Candidates…
1.1: Understand major theories and empirical research that describe the cognitive, linguistic, motivational, and sociocultural foundations of reading and writing development, processes, and components, including word recognition, language comprehension, strategic knowledge, and reading–writing connections.	• Recognize major theories of reading and writing processes and development, including first and second literacy acquisition and the role of native language in learning to read and write in a second language. • Explain language and reading development across elementary years (e.g., word recognition, language comprehension, strategic knowledge, and reading–writing connections) using supporting evidence from theory and research.[a] • Demonstrate knowledge about transfer of skills from the primary or home language (L1) to English (L2) as it affects literacy learning across these components. • Explain the research and theory about effective learning environments that support individual motivation to read and write (e.g., access to traditional print, digital, and online resources, choice, challenge, and interests).

[a]McKenna and Stahl (2009) define *reading* as including word recognition, language comprehension, and strategic knowledge (see the Glossary for their definition of *cognitive model of reading*).

The fields listed in the element are not a randomly compiled list. Rather, they are a carefully determined list of topics about which reading professionals must be knowledgeable if they are to meet the diverse instructional needs of all readers. For example, English learners have distinct linguistic and sociocultural histories that must be addressed to meet their distinct needs.

Technology

The Committee discussed the importance of technology and consulted with several researchers who study the impact of it on literacy instruction and programs. The terms *digital* and *online* are embedded in the elements and indicators of *Standards 2010* to highlight the importance of technology and the need for teachers to be knowledgeable about the use of it in their classrooms. Specifically, teachers must be able to use technology as they design, implement, and assess learning experiences for students (see International Society for Technology in Education, 2008).

Vignettes

The Middle and High School Reading Classroom Teacher Vignette

The Middle and High School Reading Classroom Teacher is a professional responsible for teaching reading at the middle or high school level. In this role, the middle or secondary reading teacher might have multiple responsibilities (see each of the Standards describing the role and function of the Middle and High School Reading Classroom Teacher).

Mr. José Rodriguez (all names are pseudonyms) is a reading teacher at Readmore Middle-Senior High School, where students are bused to school from various sections of the city. The student population is diverse, and the various ethnicities and languages enrich the school's curriculum. Mr. Rodriguez is a former social studies teacher who taught for six years before earning his master's degree, for which multiple reading classes comprised his course work. He has been a successful classroom teacher and is able to communicate with students and faculty in his new role as a reading teacher.

He understands when many of the teachers in the school tell him that they are teachers of their content, not reading teachers. It was only when he first enrolled in a course on content literacy that he began to realize the importance of knowing how to improve literacy practices with his students. Although he knew that there was a range of reading abilities within a single classroom and that using the same social studies text with all students was problematic, no one had explained how student differences and reading achievement could be addressed. Now, as a reading teacher, these past experiences, combined with what he has learned about teaching reading to adolescents, provide an important venue for the melding of literacy practices and skills. He accomplishes this by collaborating with classroom teachers, addressing their concerns, and enabling students by teaching them how to improve their reading prowess by selecting meaningful materials rather than relying primarily on programmatic materials with specified goals and outcomes.

Mr. Rodriguez has the opportunity to work with students both individually and as a group. He maintains several bookcases filled with reading materials on a wide variety of topics and reading levels, including trade books, books on tape, and a listing of electronic texts that take into account the linguistic and cultural differences of the student population. He also has classes of students who are striving to become better readers of both academic and personal reading materials. He is quick to mention a direct relationship between students' world experiences and reading comprehension when teaching adolescents. In these classes, Mr. Rodriguez administers reading assessments, plans lessons and assignments, and selects reading materials through which students can practice a skill after they have received the instruction. During and after these class sessions, he analyzes students' needs and interests and arranges these skill activities in logical order.

His classes consist of students who have a range of reading abilities, including students with difficulties. John, for example, said, "I don't read much." When Mr. Rodriguez asked John to read aloud from a passage in his book, he just stared at the words. Mr. Rodriguez asked John to read any word that he knew and was met with silence. Mr. Rodriguez gave John a list of words ranging from primer to 11th-grade difficulty with the same result: silence. Mr. Rodriguez wrote the word *cat* on a sheet of paper, and John continued to stare. Mr. Rodriguez said, "Cat." John replied, "You mean the kind that run around the house?" Mr. Rodriguez had met students like John before in his classes. These students were not "putting him on," but, rather, were enduring. Even though John was 19 years old and in the 11th grade, Mr. Rodriguez knew that he had to address the literacy challenges that John, and others with limited literacy, presented.

Throughout the school year, Mr. Rodriguez works collaboratively with the classroom teacher to learn about the various content subjects and the difficulties encountered by students in these classrooms. He offers suggestions and shares examples of strategies that the teacher can construct as adjunct aids to introduce lessons before assigning the reading of the text, during the reading of the text, and after reading the text. Mr. Rodriguez stresses the importance of having students learn *with* instead of *from* the text, which includes print and digital discourse. He is well aware that meaningful learning is preferred over rote memorization, so he demonstrates to the teacher that meaning resides within each learner, and therefore no one can learn for another. He also demonstrates how the patterns of organization (e.g., simple listing, time order, comparison and contrast, cause and effect, and problem and solution) are prevalent in these textual readings and also in the teacher's own writings.

When demonstrating strategies to the teacher, Mr. Rodriguez models how to administer some informal diagnostic instruments to students to better determine their interest and reading abilities. This modeling includes plotting each student's standardized reading test score to determine the range of reading achievement in a given class, developing and administering a cloze test from a passage of the class's textbook, creating an interest inventory that centers on the students and course content, and perhaps developing a group informal reading inventory with teacher-constructed literal, vocabulary, and interpretive questions from the assigned textbook.

Mr. Rodriguez has been invited by several teachers to come into their classrooms to demonstrate a lesson using adjunct aids, such as graphic organizers, visual literacy guides, reading/study guides, and thematic organizers. These demonstrations have piqued interest and resulted in Mr. Rodriguez working with teachers to construct their own adjunct aids. While walking down the hallway or stopping at the faculty lounge, several teachers have asked, "What can students do to learn for themselves?" On these occasions, he has met individually with these teachers and explained strategies that can be taught to their students. He showed examples and used their respective texts by demonstrating how they could teach their students how to take notes, construct electronic concept maps, and apply the SQ5R study method, and several other strategies that students can initiate on their own, so they can learn on their own.

Realizing the importance of content literacy for all members of the faculty, Mrs. Williams, the principal, asked Mr. Rodriguez if he would be willing to conduct professional development workshops. He replied, "Let's conduct a needs assessment with our faculty to see what they feel is needed to address the teaching and learning of our students." As a former classroom teacher, he feels that addressing perceived problems from within a school is far more meaningful than conducting a series of sessions that may or may not be significant or personally relevant.

Mr. Rodriguez notes that he must keep abreast of reading methods and materials and may be the only person in the school who works under the obligation to be knowledgeable about current reading practices, curricula, methods, and resources. He seeks financial support to attend and present at local, state, national, and international conferences so as to better inform his practice and personal knowledge. He values the teachers and students he works with and looks forward to learning more about literacy and its practice by pursuing an advanced reading specialist degree in the doctoral program at a nearby university.

Reading Specialist/Literacy Coach Vignettes

Reading Specialist/Literacy Coaches work at all levels, including early childhood, elementary, middle school, secondary, and adult. The following vignettes depict what these individuals might do in a school.

Notice that in some instances, Reading Specialists/Literacy Coaches have responsibilities that may require them to work with students *and* teachers. They may also have responsibility for leading efforts to develop the reading program in a school, thus the requirement that Reading Specialist/Literacy Coaches be prepared to fulfill duties across all three role definitions.

Shala: An Elementary Reading Specialist

Shala is a reading specialist working in an elementary school in a large inner-city school district. She is also known as a Title I teacher, and her position is paid for by those federal funds. Her primary responsibility is working with students who are having difficulties meeting the demands of the classroom.

To fulfill this role, she meets with teachers at the beginning of the year to discuss the students in their classrooms. This meeting occurs after teachers have an opportunity to work with their students, to get a sense of their instructional strengths and needs, and collect data via several screening tools. Shala meets with grade-level teams that make decisions to discuss the students with whom she will work, the instructional focus of her work, and various grouping options. She also talks with teachers about when she can work in their classrooms with small groups of students. In some cases, she meets with individuals or small groups in a pull-out setting.

For example, Shala plans her day so that she is in first-grade classrooms for 30 minutes each weekday when teachers are conducting differentiated instruction. In a classroom, she works with a small group of students who need additional support, while the teacher works with another small group. Shala may review a specific skill or strategy (e.g., a phonemic lesson that requires students to blend and segment) with the students or facilitate fluency practice by asking students to participate in shared or repeated reading. This schedule requires Shala to plan carefully with teachers on a consistent basis. In the afternoons, she meets with individual third-grade students who are reading below grade level to provide 20 minutes of intensive reading instruction.

Because Shala works in a school where four of the teachers are new to the profession, her principal has asked her to use some of her time to help these new teachers plan lessons, model lessons for the teachers, and help when they request support. Therefore, she may coteach or observe teachers, which is followed by conversations with the teachers to help them think about whether their instruction was effective for the students and how to improve it.

She has also found that she can provide support for these teachers in two other ways. She meets with them informally before school once a week to talk about common concerns and answer questions that they may have. Second, the new teachers, as well as other interested teachers, participate in a study group during the school's regularly scheduled professional development time, which is once a month for two hours. On the day of the professional development session, students are dismissed early, and teachers have some choice as to how they can use that time effectively to improve instruction in the school. Shala leads the group of teachers especially interested in reading instruction, who are currently reading and discussing a book about differentiated instruction.

Shala also leads efforts to inform and involve the parents and guardians of the students in this school. The school's leadership team is making a concerted effort to work with parents and guardians in ways that reinforce and support the parents' and guardians' role in promoting children's literacy development.

The above example illustrates a Reading Specialist/Literacy Coach whose primary task is working with students in the school. However, to do this job well, she must work collaboratively with teachers to enhance classroom instruction (IRA, 2000). Moreover, to enhance classroom instruction, the principal has given Shala time to coach or facilitate the work of teachers. She is involved informally in coaching through her work with leading grade-level meetings and study groups. Although coaching is not a primary responsibility, it is certainly an aspect of her position that supports student learning.

Hank: A Reading Specialist/Literacy Coach

Hank, a former middle school English teacher, is a reading specialist/literacy coach working in a large high school in a rural community. His formal title is literacy coach, and his job description indicates that his primary responsibility is to provide support for the content area teachers as they use various literacy strategies and activities to promote student learning in their respective content areas. Hank works one-on-one with teachers and also works with groups of teachers in various content disciplines.

For example, Suzie, a history teacher, indicated that her students did not seem to comprehend the material that they were assigned to read, so she wanted to learn some ways of holding class discussions that would help students critically think and talk about what they had read. Also, because there were always so many new vocabulary words essential to learning the material, she asked Hank if he could help her think of ways to build the vocabulary understanding of her students. Hank met with Suzie, talked with her about her students, and then the two of them coplanned a discussion that involved both peer conversations and a larger group discussion. Hank agreed to coteach this lesson with Suzie. He also gave her some ideas for building vocabulary before a lesson, but they agreed to focus primarily on the comprehension and discussion concerns. In this example, Hank worked with Suzie one on one, using coplanning and coteaching as coaching approaches. He knew that Suzie would also want him to observe her teaching a discussion lesson, but they would work together in future to address this particular concern.

Hank also works with groups of teachers, believing that teachers learn from each other and that one of his responsibilities is facilitating teacher sharing and networking within the teams. This also gives him an opportunity to learn from the teachers in the various content areas. He recognizes that he needs to rely on the teachers for the content knowledge that they want their students to learn. He began working with the English department, facilitating their efforts in promoting active engagement, especially in the discussions that teachers were leading in their classrooms. However, members of the social studies department, especially interested in developing better strategies for active engagement and classroom discussion, asked Hank to meet with them also. He brought both groups of teachers together, so the English teachers could share with their social studies colleagues some of the strategies that they had found successful.

The school in which Hank works just received funding from the state to promote literacy across the curriculum, so he is now holding professional development sessions in which he shares ideas that he learned at statewide meetings of literacy coaches in the funded schools. He is also leading efforts in the various content areas to review and revise the curriculum guides to infuse the literacy framework that has been adopted by his school as a result of the grant.

One of Hank's important tasks is reviewing the state assessment data from tests given to ninth and 11th graders. He discusses the results of these data with teachers at those grade levels and helps them understand what the results mean for instruction. For example, although ninth-grade students were scoring above the national mean in math computation, their scores in the story problem section were not as high. Hank and the math teachers meet to discuss ways that they can help students use a problem-solving approach for story problems. Another of Hank's tasks is scheduling classes for small groups of students whose performance on the test was poor. He works with these students for about a month, for 45 minutes twice a week, on test-taking strategies. Additionally, he shares the strategies he teaches to these students with the teachers, so they can reinforce the strategies in their classes.

Hank is a busy professional. His primary role is literacy coaching of teachers, both individually and in groups. He also works with students, either by coteaching or modeling, and sometimes teaches small groups of students, although this instruction is usually short term. Hank also has a major responsibility for leading efforts to improve the school's instructional program across all content areas by using research-based ideas about literacy learning in the curriculum.

IRA Code of Ethics

The International Reading Association is committed to the highest level of ethical conduct for all members. IRA believes that it is every member's obligation to uphold this ethical responsibility with respect to curriculum and instruction, including using technological resources; assessing, diagnosing, and evaluating; creating a literate environment; valuing diversities; communicating and interacting with families and the community; exhibiting positive dispositions; and exemplifying professionalism, including conducting research, publishing, making professional presentations, communicating and interacting with colleagues, using technology, and honestly representing oneself as a reading professional.

The IRA Code of Ethics identifies the specific ethical responsibilities for all members in each of the areas identified above. The Code is aligned with IRA Standards for Reading Professionals in order to identify ethical responsibilities related to each Standard. Any possible breaches of the IRA Code of Ethics should be referred to Association Headquarters for referral to the IRA Professional Standards and Ethics Committee for review. If any breaches are determined to have taken place, the Committee then recommends appropriate actions to the Association.

It is the obligation of all members of the International Reading Association to observe the Code of Ethics of the organization and to act accordingly so as to advance the status and prestige of the Association and of the profession as a whole.

Curriculum and Instruction

It is the ethical responsibility of all IRA members to use curriculum materials and instructional methods that:

- Are consistent with IRA position statements.

- Are based on evidence.

- Differentiate instruction to meet the individual needs of all students.

- Are free from cultural and linguistic bias.

- Represent multiple perspectives and interpretations.

- Are based on valid and reliable print and technological sources of information.

Assessing, Diagnosing, and Evaluating

It is the ethical responsibility of all IRA members to assess, diagnose, and evaluate student growth using instruments that:

- Are valid and reliable.

- Are free from cultural and linguistic bias.

- Are consistent with IRA position statements.

- Are administered in accordance with instrument specifications.

- Are interpreted in a manner consistent with the instruments' purpose.

- Are used in ways that protect the confidentiality of students and families.

Creating a Literate Environment

It is the ethical responsibility of all IRA members to create literate environments that:

- Include all students.

- Are free from bias.

- Encourage collaboration.

- Provide equitable access to books, technology-based information, and nonprint materials representing multiple levels, broad interests, and diverse cultural and linguistic backgrounds.

- Are consistent with IRA position statements.

- Are responsive to student interests, reading abilities, and backgrounds.

- Are structured to help students learn to work cooperatively and productively with others.

Exemplifying Professionalism

It is the ethical responsibility of all IRA members to exhibit professionalism by:

- Honestly representing oneself and one's work.

- Maintaining professional relationships.

- Demonstrating positive dispositions toward reading and the teaching of reading.

- Actively working to advance IRA positions, policies, and practices.

- Conducting research that is:

    - Honest.

    - Respectful of human dignity.

    - Respectful of peer input.

    - Grounded in a strong theoretical and research base.

    - Free from bias.

    - A significant contribution to understanding the reading process and the teaching of reading.

- Publishing research that is:
  - Original, and does not plagiarize previously published research.
  - Honestly represented.
  - Valid and reliable.
  - Respectful of previously published research.

Revised March 2008

Selected IRA Publications and Position Statements

Adolescent Literacy

Adolescent Literacy Instruction: Policies and Promising Practices, edited by Jill Lewis and Gary Moorman, 2007

Informed Choices for Struggling Adolescent Readers: A Research-Based Guide to Instructional Programs and Practices, by Donald D. Deshler, Annemarie Sullivan Palincsar, Gina Biancarosa, and Marnie Nair, 2007

Standards for Middle and High School Literacy Coaches, in collaboration with National Council of Teachers of English, National Council of Teachers of Mathematics, National Science Teachers Association, and National Council for the Social Studies, 2006

Assessment

Assessing Preschool Literacy Development: Informal and Formal Measures to Guide Instruction, by Billie J. Enz and Lesley Mandel Morrow, 2009

Diagnostic Literacy Assessments and Instructional Strategies: A Literacy Specialist's Resource, by Stephanie L. McAndrews, 2008

Reading Assessment: Principles and Practices for Elementary Teachers (2nd ed.), edited by Shelby J. Barrentine and Sandra M. Stokes, 2005

Understanding and Using Reading Assessment, K–12, by Peter Afflerbach, 2007

Coaching and Leadership

Coaching for Balance: How to Meet the Challenges of Literacy Coaching, by Jan Miller Burkins, 2007

Leading a Successful Reading Program: Administrators and Reading Specialists Working Together to Make It Happen, by Nancy DeVries Guth and Stephanie Stephens Pettengill, 2005

The Literacy Coach's Survival Guide: Essential Questions and Practical Answers, by Cathy A. Toll, 2005

Ready for the Classroom?: Preparing Reading Teachers With Authentic Assessments, by Mary A. Avalos, Ana Maria Pazos-Rego, Peggy D. Cuevas, Susan R. Massey, and Jeanne Shay Schumm, 2009

Content Area Learning

Building Reading Comprehension Habits in Grades 6-12: A Toolkit of Classroom Activities (2nd ed.), by Jeff Zwiers, 2010

Classroom Strategies for Interactive Learning (3rd ed.), by Doug Buehl, 2009

Comprehension Strategies for Middle Grade Learners: A Handbook for Content Area Teachers, by Charlotte Rose Sadler, 2001

Early Literacy

Creating Strategic Readers: Techniques for Developing Competency in Phonemic Awareness, Phonics, Fluency, Vocabulary, and Comprehension (2nd ed.), by Valerie Ellery, 2009

Developing Essential Literacy Skills: A Continuum of Lessons for Grades K–3, by Robin Cohen, 2008

Small-Group Reading Instruction: A Differentiated Teaching Model for Beginning and Struggling Readers (2nd ed.), by Beverly Tyner, 2009

Research and Policy

Handbook of Reading Research: Vol. 3, edited by Michael L. Kamil, Peter B. Mosenthal, P. David Pearson, and Rebecca Barr, 2000

What Research Has to Say About Reading Instruction (3rd ed.), edited by Alan E. Farstrup and S. Jay Samuels, 2002 (See also the 2009 professional development edition, which includes a facilitator's guide by Valerie Ellery and Jennifer Rosenboom.)

What Research Has to Say About Vocabulary Instruction, edited by Alan E. Farstrup and S. Jay Samuels, 2008

Struggling Readers and English Learners

Dynamic Read-Aloud Strategies for English Learners: Building Language and Literacy in the Primary Grades, by Peggy Hickman and Sharolyn D. Pollard-Durodola, 2009

English Learners: Reaching the Highest Level of English Literacy, edited by Gilbert G. García, 2003

Four Powerful Strategies for Struggling Readers, Grades 3-8: Small Group Instruction That Improves Comprehension, by Lois A. Lanning, 2008

No Quick Fix, the RTI Edition: Rethinking Literacy Programs in America's Elementary Schools, edited by Richard L. Allington and Sean A. Walmsley, 2007

Position Statements

Adolescent Literacy, 1999

Excellent Reading Teachers, 2000

High-Stakes Assessments in Reading, 1999

Investment in Teacher Preparation in the United States, 2003

Making a Difference Means Making It Different: Honoring Children's Rights to Excellent Reading Instruction, 2000

New Literacies and 21st-Century Technologies, 2009

Teaching All Children to Read: The Roles of the Reading Specialist, 2000

Using Multiple Methods of Beginning Reading Instruction, 1999

For a complete listing of all IRA publications and position statements, visit our website at www.reading.org or call 800-336-7323.

Glossary

accreditation: The process for assessing and enhancing academic and educational quality through voluntary peer review.

all readers: *See* all students.

all students: Refers to *all* students, including those who are advanced and proficient or gifted and talented, as well as those who may experience difficulty with reading and writing, such as English learners, students with learning disabilities, racially and ethnically diverse students, and students with mental disabilities.

assessment: An evaluated activity or task used by a program or unit to determine the extent to which specific learning proficiencies, outcomes, or standards have been mastered by candidates. Assessments usually include an instrument that details the task or activity and a scoring guide used to evaluate the task or activity.

assessment system: A comprehensive and integrated set of evaluation measures that provide information for use in monitoring candidate performance and managing and improving unit operations and programs for the preparation of professional educators.

balanced curriculum: A curriculum that provides teachers with a flexible framework and aligns with key factors, such as local, state, and national standards and formative and summative assessments, supports the use of traditional print, digital, and online resources, and recognizes how students learn and what they need to know.

candidates: Individuals admitted to or enrolled in programs for the initial or advanced preparation of teachers, teachers continuing their professional development, or other professional school personnel. Candidates are distinguished from students in pre-K–12 schools.

certification: The process by which a nongovernmental agency or association grants professional recognition to an individual or program that has met certain predetermined qualifications specified by that agency or association.

clinical faculty: School and higher education faculty responsible for instruction, supervision, and assessment of candidates during field experience and clinical practice.

clinical practice: Student teaching or internships that provide candidates with an intensive and extensive culminating activity. Candidates are immersed in the learning community and provided opportunities to develop and demonstrate competence in the professional roles for which they are preparing.

cognitive model of reading: As described in McKenna & Stahl (2009), Indicates that "reading is composed of three separate components. Reading comprehension, the purpose of reading, depends on (1) automatic recognition of the words in the text, (2) comprehension of the language in the text, and (3) the ability to use the strategies needed to achieve one's purpose in reading the text" (p. 8). Phonological awareness, decoding, sight words, and fluency and use of context lead to automatic word recognition. Language comprehension includes vocabulary meaning, background knowledge, and text structure. Strategic knowledge is comprised of print concepts, general purposes for reading, specific purposes for reading, and knowledge of reading strategies.

cultural background: The context of one's life experience as shaped by membership in groups based on ethnicity, race, socioeconomic status, gender, exceptionalities, language, religion, sexual orientation, and geographical area.

curriculum: The intended, enacted, assessed, and learned experiences at a specific age level or in a specific subject area. The *intended* curriculum is derived from state and national standards. The *enacted* curriculum is what is actually taught to students, and the *learned* curriculum is what students know and are able to do. The *assessed* curriculum refers to the content, skills, and strategies used.

differentiated instruction: The provision of varied learning situations, such as as whole-class, small-group, or individual instruction, to meet the needs of students at different levels of reading competence. Differentiated instruction is designed to meet the needs of each student in the classroom. It makes explicit and builds on individual students' knowledge and capabilities while teaching specific skills and strategies that are needed by each student. Differentiated instruction within the classroom includes small and flexible grouping arrangements and, at times, specific instruction for individuals.

dispositions: The values, commitments, and professional ethics that influence behaviors toward students, families, colleagues, and communities and affect student learning, motivation, and development as well as the educator's own professional growth. Dispositions are guided by beliefs and attitudes related to values, such as caring, fairness, honesty, responsibility, and social justice. For example, dispositions might include a belief that all students can learn, a vision of high and challenging standards, or a commitment to a safe and supportive learning environment.

diversity: Respect for and valuing of differences among groups and individuals related to such factors as ethnicity, race, socioeconomic status, gender, learning exceptionalities, geographic area, physical abilities, language, religion, sexual orientation, and political affiliations and other ideologies.

elementary grades: Most often includes grades K–6. However, in some school district configurations, elementary grades may include K–8.

elements of Standards: The major components of each Standard that are described in the rubrics and the explanations that accompany the Standards. *Standards* is the term that describes the primary level, and *elements* is the secondary level.

English learners: Children and adults who are learning English as a second or additional language. This term may apply to learners across levels of proficiency in English. English learners may also be referred to as English-language learners, non–English-speaking, limited English proficient, nonnative speakers, and language-minority students. A majority of students identified as limited English proficient in U.S. schools are native born (U.S. Department of Education, 2007).

ethnicity: Physical and cultural characteristics that make a social group distinctive and may include, but are not limited to, national origin, ancestry, language, shared history, traditions, values, and symbols—all of which contribute to a sense of distinctiveness among members of an ethnic group.

evidence-based education: The integration of best available empirical evidence with professional wisdom in making decisions about how to deliver instruction. Empirical evidence is scientifically based evidence in which objective measures of performance are used to compare, evaluate, and monitor progress. Professional wisdom is the judgment that individuals acquire through experience and is reflected through numerous ways, including the effective identification and incorporation of local circumstances into instruction.

exceptionalities: A physical, mental, or emotional condition, including gifted and talented abilities, that requires individualized instruction or other educational support or services.

field experiences: A variety of early and ongoing field-based opportunities in which candidates may observe, assist, tutor, instruct, and/or conduct research. Field experiences may occur in off-campus settings such as schools, community centers, or homeless shelters.

full-time faculty: Employees of a higher education institution with full-time assignments with the professional education unit, who include instructors, professors at different ranks, administrators, and professional support personnel.

indicators of the Standards: The components of each of the elements of a Standard that describe performance at the end of a preparation program that must be met to meet the Standard.

initial teacher preparation: Programs at baccalaureate or postbaccalaureate levels that prepare candidates for their first teaching license.

internship: Generally, postlicensure or graduate clinical practice under the supervision of clinical faculty; sometimes refers to the preservice clinical experience.

licensure: The official recognition by a state governmental agency that an individual has met certain qualifications specified by the state and is, therefore, approved to practice in an occupation as a professional. (Some state agencies call their licenses *certificates* or *credentials*.)

literacy: The ability to read, write, speak, listen, view, visually represent, and think in order to communicate and contribute to society.

literate: The ability to read, write, and have knowledge and appreciation of literature.

middle grades: Most often refers to grades 6–8. However, many districts may use 5–8, 7–8, or 7–9 as middle-grade designations. *See* secondary grades.

new literacies: Information and communication technologies, such as cellular telephones, personal computers, MP3 players, and the Internet, that shape new forms of reading and writing, including the skills, strategies, and dispositions necessary to successfully use and adapt to the rapidly changing information and communication technologies and contexts that continually emerge in our world.

off-campus programs: Programs offered by a unit on sites other than the main campus. Off-campus programs may be offered in the same state, in other states, or in countries other than the United States.

other professional school personnel: Educators who provide professional services other than teaching in schools, who include, but are not limited to, principals, reading specialists and supervisors, school library media specialists, school psychologists, school superintendents, and instructional technology specialists.

partner schools: Public and private schools with which the program coordinator collaborates in designing field experiences, practical assignments, and internships in reading for candidates under the supervision of school and program faculty. These field experiences and assignments can occur both in the candidates' schools and in other school settings.

part-time faculty: Employees of a higher education institution who have less than a full-time assignment in the professional education unit. Some part-time faculty are full-time employees of the college or university, with a portion of their assignments in the professional education unit. Other part-time faculty are not full-time employees of the institution and are commonly considered adjunct faculty.

pedagogical content knowledge: The interaction of subject matter and effective teaching strategies to help students learn the subject matter. It requires a thorough understanding of the content to teach it in multiple ways, drawing on the cultural backgrounds and prior knowledge and experiences of the students.

pedagogical knowledge: The general concepts, theories, and research about effective teaching, regardless of content areas.

performance-based assessment: A comprehensive assessment through which candidates demonstrate their proficiencies in subject, professional, and pedagogical knowledge and skills, including their abilities to have positive effects on student learning.

professional community: Full- and part-time faculty, including clinical faculty, in the professional education unit, or other units of the college or university, as well as pre-K–12 practitioners, candidates, and others involved in professional education.

professional development: Opportunities for educators to develop new knowledge and skills through inservice education, conference attendance, sabbatical leave, summer leave, intra- and interinstitutional visitations, fellowships, job-embedded coaching, and so forth.

professional education faculty: Individuals employed by a college or university, including graduate teaching assistants, who teach one or more courses in education, provide services to candidates (e.g., advising), supervise clinical experiences, or administer some portion of the unit.

program: A planned sequence of courses and experiences for preparing pre-K–12 teachers and other professional school personnel. These courses and experiences sometimes lead to a recommendation for a state license to work in schools.

reading development: The course of change in an individual's reading processes from their emergence in reading to learning the more mature skills and abilities of the competent reader.

Response to Intervention: A U.S. initiative that encourages schools to provide early, effective assistance to children who have difficulty with learning. Response to Intervention was also designed to function as a data-based process of diagnosing learning disabilities. This method can be used at the group and individual levels.

rubrics: Written and shared criteria for judging performance that indicate the qualities by which levels of performance can be differentiated and that anchor judgments about the degree of success on a candidate's assessment.

scholarly work: Research and other creative work, including presentations, exhibits, and demonstrations, that contribute to knowledge building.

school faculty: Licensed practitioners in pre-K–12 schools who provide instruction, supervision, and direction for candidates during field-based assignments.

schools: Public and private pre-K–12 institutions that provide instruction in a prescribed curriculum delivered by licensed practitioners. Candidates are placed in local schools for pre–student teaching experiences related to the reading program.

secondary grades: Grades 7–12, depending on school district configurations. *See* middle grades.

specialized professional associations: The national organizations that represent teachers, professional education faculty, and other school personnel who teach a specific subject matter (e.g., mathematics or social studies), teach students at a specific developmental level (i.e., early childhood, elementary, middle level, or secondary), teach students with specific needs (e.g., bilingual education or special education), administer schools (e.g., principals or superintendents), or provide services to students (e.g., school counselors or school psychologists). Many of these associations are constituent members of NCATE and have standards for both students in schools and candidates preparing to work in schools.

standards: Written expectations for meeting a specified level of performance. Standards exist for the content that pre-K–12 students should know at a certain age or grade level.

state approval: Governmental activity requiring specific professional development education programs within a state to meet standards of quality, so program graduates will be eligible for licensing.

struggling readers: Refers to any student experiencing difficulty in learning to read and write. The term describes behavior and does not imply any specific causes or identify students as belonging to a specific category, such as having a particular learning disability. Further, not all students identified as English learners are struggling readers; neither are all students who are racially or ethnically diverse.

students: Children and youth attending pre-K–12 schools, as distinguished from teacher candidates.

student teaching: Preservice clinical practice for candidates preparing to teach.

supervised practicum experience: A supervised practicum has a supervisor who is licensed in the area that he or she is observing and has the appropriate credentials (*see* the Teacher Educator Candidates column in the Standards matrixes). A portion of the supervised practicum experience should require working with students who struggle with reading and include collaborative and coaching experiences with teachers. Such experiences may occur in reading/literacy clinics or school-based programs. Practicum experiences may also be embedded in course assignments that require classroom-based interventions; these may be supervised through lesson plans, conferences, site visits, videotapes, and so forth.

technology: *See* new literacies.

vignette: A short, impressionistic story that gives a particular insight into the multiple roles of a reading professional and the environment in which he or she teaches.

References

Frost, S., & Bean, R. (2006). *Qualifications for literacy coaches: Achieving the gold standard.* Retrieved May 17, 2010, from Literacy Coaching Clearinghouse website: www.literacycoachingonline.org/briefs/LiteracyCoaching.pdf

International Reading Association. (2000). *Teaching all children to read: The roles of the reading specialist* [Position statement]. Newark, DE: Author. Available: www.reading.org/General/AboutIRA/PositionStatements/ReadingSpecialistPosition.aspx

International Reading Association. (2004). *The role and qualifications of the reading coach in the United States* [Position statement]. Newark, DE: Author. Available: www.reading.org/General/AboutIRA/PositionStatements/ReadingCoachPosition.aspx

International Reading Association. (2009). *Response to Intervention: Guiding principles for educators from the International Reading Association.* Newark, DE: Author. Available: www.reading.org/General/AboutIRA/Governance/Committees/RTICommission.aspx

International Society for Technology in Education. (2008). *The ISTE national educational technology standards (NETS-T) and performance indicators for teachers.* Eugene, OR: Author. Available: www.iste.org/Content/NavigationMenu/NETS/ForTeachers/2008Standards/NETS_for_Teachers_2008.htm

McKenna, M.C., & Stahl, K.A.D. (2009). *Assessment for reading instruction* (2nd ed.). New York: Guilford.

National Council for Accreditation of Teacher Education. (2010). Policy on guidelines for writing and approval of SPA standards. In *SASB policies and procedures handbook* (pp. 5–51). Washington, DC: Specialty Areas Studies Board, National Council for Accreditation of Teacher Education.

Rothman, R., Slattery, J.B., Vranek, J.L., & Resnick, L.B. (2002). *Benchmarking and alignment of standards and testing* (CSE Technical Report 566). Los Angeles: National Center for Research on Evaluation, Standards, and Student Testing.

Status of Reading Instruction Institute & International Reading Association. (2007). *Teaching reading well: A synthesis of the International Reading Association's research on teacher preparation for reading instruction.* Newark, DE: International Reading Association. Available: www.reading.org/Libraries/SRII/teaching_reading_well.sflb.ashx

U.S. Department of Education, Office of Elementary and Secondary Education. (2007). *Assessment and accountability for recently arrived and former limited English proficient (LEP) students: Non-regulatory guidance.* Washington, DC: Author.

Wiggins, G., & McTighe, J. (2007). *Schooling by design: Mission, action, and achievement.* Alexandria, VA: Association for Supervision and Curriculum Development.